Trying to Get Toothpaste Back Into the Tube

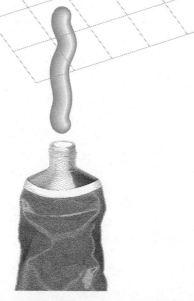

Trying to Get Toothpaste Back Into the Tube

Making Choices You Don't Have to Undo

Lorraine Peterson

BETHANY HOUSE PUBLISHERS

Minneapolis, Minnesota 55438

Inside illustrations by Paula Becker

Published by Bethany House Publishers
A Ministry of Bethany Fellowship, Inc.
11300 Hampshire Avenue South
Minneapolis, Minnesota 55438

Printed in the United States of America

Library of Congress Cataloging-in-Publication Data

Peterson, Lorraine.
    Trying to get toothpaste back into the tube / Lorraine Peterson.
       p.   cm.
    Summary: Examines moral issues facing teenagers today, including sexuality, integrity, and hard work; and discusses setting inner goals.
    1. Teenagers—Religious life. 2. Teenagers—Conduct of life.
3. Christian life—1960–
[1. Conduct of life. 2. Christian life.]
I. Title.
BV4531.2.P4888   1993
248.8'3—dc20   93-12146
ISBN 1-55661-315-6   CIP
                                                 AC

Dedication

I'd like this book to be a memorial to my father, Bertil Peterson, who died suddenly of a heart attack in September 1992. He and my stepmother, Lorraine, have always been very supportive of my writing career. His enthusiasm, faithfulness to responsibility, and simple trust that God always knows best have influenced my life. From him I learned to respect the biblical values that have guarded my life and have become part of this book.

LORRAINE PETERSON was born in Red Wing, Minnesota, grew up on a farm near Ellsworth, Wisconsin, and now resides in Ciudad Juárez, Mexico. She received her B.A. (in history) from North Park College in Chicago, and has taken summer courses from the University of Minnesota and the University of Mexico in Mexico City.

Lorraine has taught high school and junior high. She has been an advisor to nondenominational Christian clubs in Minneapolis public schools, has taught teenage Bible studies, and continues to work with young people. She has written several bestselling devotional books for teens:

Anybody Can Be Cool, But Awesome Takes Practice
Dying of Embarrassment & Living to Tell About It
Falling Off Cloud Nine and Other High Places
If God Loves Me, Why Can't I Get My Locker Open?
If the Devil Made You Do It, You Blew It!
If You Really Trust Me, Why Can't I Stay Out Later?
Lord, I Haven't Talked to You Since the Last Crisis, But . . .
Please Give Me Another Chance, Lord
Radical Advice From the Ultimate Wise Guy
Real Characters in the Making
Trying to Get Toothpaste Back Into the Tube
Why Isn't God Giving Cash Prizes?

Preface

Society has become crazed with pleasure and comfort, making it hard for young people to choose the narrow way that leads to life eternal. Few even think of tomorrow, much less the life hereafter. Discipline, self-control, respect for authority, unselfishness, chastity, concern for others, and following God aren't valued in secular society. Some young people have role models who are as guilty as most teens of living for instant gratification. Sadly, the sum of many bad decisions is a dysfunctional population—emotionally wounded, easily discouraged, and morally impotent. Reversing monumental mistakes is like trying to get toothpaste back into the tube.

This book is designed to help teens see the possibility and importance of making excellent choices. They need to know the power of the Holy Spirit is available to enable them to make right decisions. Practical, scriptural advice shows them how choosing God's way at every turn is a worthwhile future investment. My prayer is that young people who read what I have written will be encouraged to seek God's will in every detail of daily life—choosing to go first-class.

I'm grateful to God for His love, His care, and His guidance. When I hear a sermon that summarizes what I'm trying to put down on paper, receive material in the mail on the subject I'm writing about, or get a good idea as a direct answer to prayer, I am reminded that God deserves all the credit for this book. His faithfulness is fantastic. He has also surrounded me with supportive people. I'm grateful to my talented and easy-to-work-with editor, David Hazard, for suggesting that I write this book and, as usual, improving on the original manuscript. I appreciate the constant encouragement of my roommate, Tere Rodriquez; my sister, Lynn; and my brother-in-law, Earl; as well as nieces and nephews Beth, Brett, Kaari, and Kirk.

Contents

1
You Are What You Choose

Only Robots Can Avoid Making Decisions

Todd found that fourth-hour biology bored him to death—until Nadia walked in with an "admit slip." She was the most beautiful creature he'd ever laid eyes on: long blond hair, stunning hazel eyes, a perfect body. She could have been on the cover of a magazine. And it was obvious that she "noticed" him, too. At the end of the first week she asked if he'd help her with biology homework.

They met after school, and he drove her to McDonald's. Everything went so smoothly he could hardly believe it. He always liked the booth in the corner, and that's where she wanted to sit. He was hoping she enjoyed football so he could invite her to the Friday night game, and at that very moment she came out with, "Does this school have a good football team? I hope so, because I love to go to the games." It was too unbelievable.

Todd had an eerie feeling. His mind seemed to be controlling hers. Maybe it was all coincidence. He decided to test it out.

Mentally, he programmed her to kiss him just when their order came and to say that her hobby was collecting exotic butterflies. . . . And in another moment her smile turned into a leering, robotic grin. . . .

The buzz of the alarm clock shook Todd out of his dream-turned-nightmare. Reflecting over the strange experience in his dream, he realized he'd never want to date a robot—no matter how gorgeous she was. He really wanted to get to know some sharp girl with her own unique personality who'd *choose* to love him.

God must feel the same way. He created you with the ability to decide for yourself whether or not you wish to love and obey Him. He will never force you to think a certain way or change your actions, even though He has the power to do so. But to guide you to himself, God has woven into the universe consequences for your choices—rewards and punishments we can feel in the here-and-now and in the eternal life to come.

Some people argue and say, "God already knows the choices I'll make—so how can He let me get into a tempting situation and then punish me for choosing wrong? Isn't that just a setup?"

Dr. Walter Martin explained it like this. We get to push the buttons on God's preprogrammed computer. Each choice brings certain consequences and God knows ahead of time what we'll choose.

Because God made the computer, nothing is outside His control—but at the same time we get to exercise our free will!

Other people say, "Even if I sin, I can ask God to forgive me, and that's that. Right?"

It's true that God completely forgives sin and wrong choices. But forgiveness does not erase the *scars*. God knows that choosing worldly friends, marrying the wrong person, or dedicating our lives to a wrong cause will cause us great suffering. Still He values our freedom so much that He did not make us robots.

☛ Your Most Important Choice

Accepting or rejecting Christ is a choice between heaven and hell—a choice between a life of purpose and fulfillment, or one of frustration. He wants to live His supernatural life through you and me, and He invites us to spend a glorious eternity with Him. Like me, you're at complete liberty to decide what you'll do with His offer.

In order for Christ to come into your life and transform you:

1. You must agree with God's definition of sin. And you must be willing to plug in to His power to change your ways in order to conform to His commandments.
2. You must confess your wrongdoing and acknowledge that only the blood of Jesus Christ—no "good works" that you can do—will be able to make your sinful heart clean.
3. You need to be willing to make a permanent commitment of your life to Jesus Christ, giving Him the right to call the shots. (It's not a try-it-for-thirty-days-and-if-you-don't-like-it-your-money-will-be-refunded proposition.)
4. Finally, you have to pray to invite Jesus to come into your heart to forgive your sins and make changes in the way you

think, act, and plan your future.

If you haven't taken this awesome step, you will find this book of little value. But you can talk to God right now, give yourself fully to Him, and receive the new life He longs to give you.

☛ Your New Life Will Be Full of Decisions

So often we face unchangeable situations. In these areas where we can't chart our own course, we're often presented with a full range of responses. Some are guaranteed to make things even worse. Others will merely keep things the way they are, or postpone facing reality. Even the choices that will bring improvement can be categorized into: good, better, and best. The goals you can reach in life will not be determined so much by the raw materials you have to work with—intelligence, appearance, emotional make-up, family background, and circumstances—as by your *choices*. You are, and will be, what you choose.

One of the smartest things you can do is to *reject* the popular beliefs that

1. You're a product of pure chance evolved through some purpose- less process.
2. You might just as well flow with the current (of doing what comes naturally, of giving in to peer pressure, of taking the eas- iest path) since whatever will be will be.
3. You should look within yourself to find truth and meaning in life because there are no absolute values or ways of doing things that hold the key to satisfaction in life.

These ideas are completely false. There is a God who has given us His guidelines for successful living in His Book. The only insurance policy against full-time failure is to make wise decisions based on God's Word. You can choose—so why not decide to make excellent choices?

Think: *Quality*

Ask for Advice

"Don't tell me what to do," *and* "I'll make up my own mind." These attitudes reflect an awareness that it's wrong for other people to treat us like robots. No one has the right to control our thoughts or actions. Yes, it's natural to outgrow our childhood dependence on adults—but for many young people this is often accompanied by exaggerated expressions of independence. Rebellion against wise restraints can result in disaster. Like a train, you're only truly free to function well while you stay on the tracks. God made limits for us, His creatures, because He loves us and wants us to enjoy our stay on this earth.

Proverbs tells us: "Plans fail for lack of counsel, but with many advisors they succeed" (15:22). If you want to make excellent choices, you can begin by seeking the advice of older people who are dedicated Christians, people who are so secure in Jesus that they won't be offended if you don't take the route they propose. When a big decision faces you, learn to state the facts honestly and clearly, and listen attentively to counsel. After you've talked with several mature Christians, pray and ask God to direct your final choice.

▨ Dare to Be Different

When you buy a cheap shirt or blouse, you can be sure you'll blend in with lots of other people who bought the same thing. But the most expensive clothing is unique—nobody else shows up at a royal reception wearing a dress identical to that of Queen Elizabeth!

Because Jesus lives within, you are different. You can stand out from the crowd, because your attitudes and actions are different. God has given you His Holy Spirit to provide that incredible power necessary for you to live a truly extraordinary life.

Satan's portable prison is made out of conformity-cement and become-a-carbon-copy bars. Even Christians can choose to live in jail by deciding to be like everyone else. Then they fall for temptation, when they could be champions for right living. Why not break out of the prison of wanting to be like everyone else and become that unique and impressive personality that God created you to be?

▨ Resist Recycling

Recycling cans, bottles, and paper is fine. But once a life is ruined or destroyed, the consequences can be devastating. Some people shrug and say, "Every kid sows some wild oats," or "He'll settle down someday," or "She's only sixteen. What can you expect of her?" It's pretty easy to fall into the I'm-young-so-what-I-do-doesn't-matter way of thinking. To make matters worse, the devil is promoting a live-for-today-forget-about-the-future pitch. Whatever makes you high or happy or homogenized with the crowd goes, no matter how terrible the long-range consequences may be.

We are led to believe that "Look before you leap," "Think ahead," "Obey God's commandments," or "Live for Jesus" are leftovers from some ancient ice age and the surest way to commit social suicide. "Nothing off limits" and "everything goes" is painted as the modern lifestyle. This easy-sleazy mentality has been hanging around for hundreds of years. *Two thousand* years ago, people said: "Let's eat and drink, for tomorrow we die!" This foolish philosophy has destroyed millions of lives. (Funny, but that's exactly what Satan has in mind. . . .)

The truth is that we can follow God's Word and continually make excellent choices. We can use our time, money, and energy to the best advantage. We can develop wholesome and satisfying relationships with relatives, employees, and friends. Every young person can live in such a way that there is little or no waste to recycle.

☛ Learn From Your Mistakes

Even if your goal is to follow God and you try to choose wisely, you'll make some wrong turns—that is part of being humans who are growing from spiritual blindness into clearer understanding of God and what He wants for us. When you fail, you can learn from your errors and become even wiser. There are two extremes to avoid. If you automatically defend everything you do, you'll keep repeating your foolish and sinful actions. On the other hand, if you permit a mistake to derail your joy and confidence, you'll waste a lot of time being depressed and discouraged.

How should you handle failure? Those who make it to the finals in ice-skating competitions have mastered the art of recovering quickly from a fall. They go on skating just as gracefully as before. You too can learn from your mistakes.

The guidance in this book will introduce you to the awesome adventure of learning how to cooperate with God in designing a fantastic future. How? By learning how to make *excellent* choices, no matter what!

2

A Winning Attitude Is Based on Truth

Who Is Your God?

Are you worshiping a false god?

"Wait a minute," you may be thinking, "that's an insult. I'm not some aborigine out of the pages of *National Geographic* who's into pagan rituals. I believe in the one true God."

Do you? Inventing your own god is a lot easier than you might think. You and I can get into heavy-duty trouble if we replace the God of the Bible with a god who is more to our "liking."

Who *is* God? What is His character? Some people think God can be anybody they want Him to be—Santa Claus, or a sleepy old grandpa in the sky. But God is a Person, and He is who He is. You can't just determine that it's just too unpleasant to believe, for example, that God will allow some people to go to hell. You can't decide that God won't mind if you break a few of His commandments, or that He is amused at human selfishness. You have to get the facts about God straight. God is not a fantasy you can toy with. You must rely on the Bible—the book which reveals what He is like—to form your concept of Him.

▶ Avoiding Chris, Cassandra, Carla, and Other Godmakers

Chris is the classic "chameleon Christian." He changes his conduct and values as the situation requires. He can fit in at church, fully enjoying all the youth activities—even Bible studies. But his pastor would black out if he knew what kinds of things Chris does with his school friends. Chris has a lot of curiosity, and he loves to be where the action is. So he parties with his buddies and checks out the music, movies, and magazines they're all talking about. He wants the *benefits* of Christianity—plus all that the world has to offer. Popularity is his priority and he always seems to be well-liked by everyone.

To Chris, God is a kind of easygoing coach who, like everyone else, is glad to see him whenever he shows up. Secretly, he feels God is lucky to have such a popular guy on His "side," and that He'll gladly stretch the rules a little just to have Chris on His team.

Chris lives as if some aspects of the truth about God did not exist. "Don't you know that friendship with the world is hatred toward God?" (James 4:4) is not for him. He tunes out Jesus' voice when he hears the scripture, "If anyone would come after me, he must deny himself and take up his cross daily and follow me" (Luke 9:23). And he wishes that the warning "everyone who wants to have a godly life in Christ Jesus will be persecuted" (2 Timothy 3:12) were not in the Bible.

Chris's false god does not say things like, "Be holy, because I am holy" (1 Peter 1:16). Or "Do not worship any other god, for the Lord, whose name is Jealous, is a jealous God" (Exodus 34:14). Sure, a grown man has a right to be jealous when his wife flirts with another man, because she belongs to him. But Chris doesn't get it—that God can't stand our putting anything else before Him because it messes *us* up, as well as His whole creation.

In Chris's brand of "salvation" he doesn't see himself as a person who has sinned and fallen short of the glory of God (Romans 3:23). He doesn't concern himself with being a "new creature in Christ" (2 Corinthians 5:17). Chris's true god is *popularity*. Almost without realizing it, he has adjusted his image of God so he can do whatever he wants without feeling guilty.

On the other hand, there is Cassandra. . . .

Cassandra always looks a bit worried—kind of like she's afraid she might fall off an invisible tightrope she's walking on. She's so concerned that she'll say the wrong thing that she rarely talks about her faith. To her, most leisure time activities fall into the category of sin. She tries hard to be helpful—so hard that she sometimes makes a nuisance of herself. She's afraid God will *zap* her the moment she blows it. She imagines Him to be rather like Zeus with his thunderbolts, ready to strike her down whenever she does something wrong. Her god requires *extra* good deeds to cover up her mistakes, and he never forgets her past failures.

Cassandra suffers from low self-esteem because she can never measure up to what her "god" demands. She's so insecure she accepts each new rule and prohibition people lay on her. If someone told her that wearing high heels or owning a pet cat was a sin, she'd accept it without thinking.

Cassandra never stops to consider scriptures like these:

> From everlasting to everlasting the Lord's love is with those who fear him. (Psalm 103:17)

> If we confess our sins, he is faithful and just and will forgive us our sins and purify us from all unrighteousness. (1 John 1:9)

"Salvation Cassandra-style" is something you work for. You can never be sure you've done enough to attain it. She cannot grasp Ephesians 2:8–9: "For it is by grace you have been saved, through faith and this is not from yourselves, it is the gift of God—not by works, so that no one can boast." In fact, self-righteousness is her true god. Life means making all the sacrifices necessary to appease this tyrant, and it means working hard to be better than anyone else in order to get on His good side.

Carla has never liked it when someone told her what to do. Just the existence of a rule makes her think about breaking it. Authority figures have always given her problems. Intelligent and independent, she likes to do her own thing.

Carla's god lets his creatures do as they like. She figures that her attitudes can all be accounted for by one simple statement: "That's the way I am." And in her mind she adds, *Besides, God made me like this, so it's His problem.* Because she values self above all things, she's really her own god.

Although she hasn't torn these words out of her Bible, she might as well have: "He [or she] who rebels against the authority is rebelling against what God has instituted, and those who do so will bring judgment on themselves" (Romans 13:2). "Obey your leaders and submit to their authority" (Hebrews 13:17).

Carla's idea of salvation doesn't include submitting her life to Jesus, and she's never confronted Matthew 7:21: "Not everyone who says to me, 'Lord, Lord,' will enter the kingdom of heaven, but only he who does the will of my Father who is in heaven."

Getting Acquainted With the Real God

Corey got tired of living for himself. His life was a disaster and he knew it. As he read the words, "Jesus answered, 'I am the way and the truth and the life. No one comes to the Father except through me' "(John 14:6), he believed them. When he came to Jesus, he surrendered his life completely. He fully understood that accepting Jesus meant not only receiving forgiveness of sins: It included permitting Jesus to come into his heart to live His life through Corey's physical body. Knowing that Jesus lives inside him, Corey is aware of the fact that he can plug in to supernatural power to overcome the sin and the bad habits he acquired. Whatever he found in the Bible he was determined to obey—even if his friends thought he was crazy and his family didn't understand. He realized that the Jesus who healed the blind man and walked on the water could give him the miracles he needed to follow God's commandments. And things like getting along with Butch Miller, handing in his homework every day, and changing the way he used his spare time required strength beyond his own.

Because of his submissive attitude, Corey doesn't need to invent a god who thinks sick-o movies are okay, or one who looks the other way if he goes too far with his girlfriend. He lets God be exactly who He is—a God who loves and saves sinners but punishes sin. A God who sets limits for our own good. A God so great that we are at a loss to understand all His ways. A God who deserves our total obedience. Corey takes Scripture at face value and receives the power of the Holy Spirit to conform his life to the commands of the God of the Bible.

☑ Are You in the False God Construction Business?

Have you changed your image of God to accommodate wrong actions or rebellious attitudes? Honestly answer the following questions.

1. Have I tried to squeeze God into a mold I've made for Him?

_____

2. How is my god different from the God of the Bible? _____

_____

_____

3. What activities or attitudes do I try to rationalize—although deep in my heart I know they're wrong? _____

_____

_____

4. Am I honestly willing to take a hard look at some areas in my life with the intention of making an obedience commitment to God that will make big changes in my life? _____

_____

_____

☑ And Lord I Promise ...

Because the God who is there—the real Lord of the universe—requires things of us, part of Christian commitment is making promises to Him. The Bible records many instances in which people made specific declarations of their intentions to follow God.

Joshua challenged the people: "Choose for yourselves this day whom you will serve." When the Israelites answered, "We will serve the Lord," he explained that they were all witnesses to this promise and he set up a special stone to help them remember their vow.

New converts in Ephesus wanted to declare that they would

never again return to witchcraft. "A number who had practiced sorcery brought their scrolls together and burned them publicly." They even determined the value of the books they had burned. It was their way of making a statement about their new life resolutions.

Isaiah heard the voice of the Lord saying, "Whom shall I send? And who will go for us?" He replied, "Here am I. Send me." And God used Isaiah as His mouthpiece for the rest of his life.

Great Christians throughout the ages have made vows to God. The world has changed because David Wilkerson promised God he was willing to sell his TV and spend his viewing time in prayer. Hudson Taylor was willing to go to China, even though it meant breaking up with the girl he loved. Corrie Ten Boom decided to praise God even in a Nazi concentration camp, and thousands have been changed by her faithfulness.

Pledges that we make to God concerning "little things" shape our lives. Every time we come to a crossroads, we must decide whether or not we'll obey God. The importance of each decision can be determined only as we look back. Don't underestimate the importance of small decisions. Your promises to God will determine to a great degree your growth in the Christian life.

Keeping those promises, however, is much more important than making them. "When you make a vow to God, do not delay in fulfilling it. He has no pleasure in fools; fulfill your vow. It is better not to vow than to make a vow and not fulfill it" (Ecclesiastes 5:4–5). If you give your word to God, consider the contract binding.

3
Give Him a Piece of Your Time

What Do You Have Planned for the Weekend?

Relaxation and fun are part of God's plan for you. If your hectic schedule includes nothing but school, study, and work, your body will begin to register complaints. Headaches and stomach problems are probably the most common. When God set up the rules that He meant for the Israelites to use in forming a model society, there were several national celebrations throughout the year. Sometimes the whole population went on vacation. All of these had a spiritual emphasis along with such things as feasting, camping out, and gift-giving. Who knows? Since there were many young warriors and hunters, they may even have enjoyed some sporting events. (Anyone for a sling-shot contest? Javelin throw?)

The Bible also tells us it is necessary and good to work. There are many warnings against laziness. Failure to do your share of the work around the house, or keep up with studies, or help out at church results in having too much time on your hands. Boredom can lead to misuse of leisure time.

Today we have an infinite variety of possibilities to fill our spare momemts—music, movies, magazines, MTV. Many of the possibilities set before us can be damaging to our spiritual health. Other choices will keep us in good shape physically, increase brain power, widen our circle of friends, and enable us to return to our work refreshed. How do we choose? Fortunately, the Bible gives us some very helpful principles.

☑ Don't Try to Find Out More About Evil

The devil is carrying out a very successful advertising campaign, branding people as abnormal if they're afraid to try all the world has to offer. To the worldly mind, nothing is off limits. Experiencing every possible high is supposed to be sophisticated. Purity and innocence are considered old-fashioned, un-cool, and impossible.

Although it wears a different mask, that strategy—to call what is good stupid—is as old as Adam and Eve. The devil appealed to her using the false argument that it was okay to disobey God. Eve was led to believe that if she experienced sin as well as obedience, she'd widen her horizons and become as wise as God! Eve ate from the tree of the knowledge of good and evil—but she would have been infinitely better off without all her new insight about life. If you don't do drugs, have sex outside of marriage, rebel against authority, or stray from God, consider all that you'll "miss out" on: addiction, heartbreak, broken relationships, and a lot of angry turmoil. Be smart—and recognize that there are some things you can live without. Be intelligent enough to be different.

The apostle Paul had some pretty good reasons for writing, "I want you to be wise about what is good, and innocent about what is evil" (Romans 16:19). And, "In regard to evil be infants, but in your thinking be adults" (1 Corinthians 14:20). Following your inquisitiveness into learning about all the sordid details of life could cost an awful lot. (With an emphasis on awful!)

On January 23, 1989, Dr. James Dobson had an interview with serial-killer Ted Bundy, who was guilty of raping and murdering many women and girls. Sentenced to die the next morning, he had asked for the chance to tell his story in order to warn young people against movies and magazines featuring sex and violence. He also hoped to promote legislation banning such material. Having accepted Christ as his Savior and having confessed to his crime, Bundy wanted the last day of his life to make a good impact on society.

Answering Dr. Dobson's questions, he related the following: He grew up in a good Christian home where he was never abused physically or emotionally. Because his social life, school performance, and family relationships all appeared to be normal, no one suspected his secret sin. It all began at the age of twelve or thirteen when he was introduced to soft-core pornography. It incited his imagination and gradually he began to seek out the really graphic material that connected sex and violence. His fantasies became more and more real, finally causing him to explode to the point where he began to act them out in real life. Ted Bundy insisted that pornography and crime are connected and that pornography must be banned.

What worried Bundy was that the violent and sexually explicit movies so easily accessible today weren't even shown in X-rated movie theaters when he was a teenager. The fact that men he met in prison, who were guilty of crimes similar to his, had all used pornography further convinced him of its evil effects. In addition, an FBI investigation of serial-killers revealed that the one thing all had in common was an addiction to pornography.

Why on earth should you repeat the experiment just to see if Ted Bundy knew what he was talking about? Why try to prove that you are made of tougher stuff than he was? Why play Russian roulette? There are a lot of things you'd be better off *not* knowing.

☛ Constantly Subject Your Choices to the Test of Scripture and the Advice of Mature, Godly Christians

Cockroaches, crooks, and cowards all like dark places and prefer that no one investigate their actions. Whenever you become overly defensive about something in your life, take it as a warning sign. And when you react to a particular Bible verse with a long excuse that sidesteps the Scriptural meaning, or when you purposely tell only half the truth, or when you try to cover your tracks—you're headed for big trouble.

Scripture is very clear about how you should live in relation to evil: "Avoid every kind of evil" (1 Thessalonians 5:22). The apostle Paul describes his actions this way: "For we are taking pains to do what is right, not only in the eyes of the Lord but also in the eyes of men" (2 Corinthians 8:21). That's the biblical standard.

The *acid test* for your inner attitude was clearly described by Jesus, the Light of the World: "Everyone who does evil hates the light, and will not come into the light for fear that his deeds will be exposed. But whoever lives by the truth comes into the light, so that it may be seen plainly that what he has done has been done through God" (John 3:20, 21).

Some practical application questions include the following:

1. Am I doing something that makes me feel uncomfortable about going to church? _____ If so, what? _____

2. Am I doing something I want to keep hidden from other Christians? _____ If so, what? _____

3. Is there a Bible verse I don't want to face squarely because of my actions? _____ Which verse? _____

4. Is there something I'm unwilling to stop doing even if according to Scripture it's wrong? _____ What is it? _____

Just remember, this is a formula for misery: trying to straddle the fence and live a double life. Turn everything over to Jesus, so you can stop playing games and walk out into the light of God's freedom.

Some people use another approach to disobeying God's commandments. They take the attitude that it-might-not-be-right-for-you-but-it-doesn't-hurt-me-a-bit. True, even good Christians can differ on whether it's okay to engage in certain activities. But one spiritual principle remains constant: You must be honest with God, yourself, and others—and you must be willing to stop any activity that comes between you and God.

"For lack of guidance a nation falls, but many advisers make victory sure" (Proverbs 11:14). "A wise son heeds his father's instruction, but a mocker does not listen to rebuke" (Proverbs 13:1). And just in case you didn't get the point, "He who hates correction is stupid" (Proverbs 12:1).

If you're not open to counsel offered by good Christians or willing to prayerfully consider the reasons given against participating in certain activities, you've probably got an idol on your hands—some person or activity that pushes God into second place.

Take secular rock music for example. In their book *Why Knock Rock?*, Dan and Steve Peters point out that any music with unwholesome lyrics, advertised by disgusting graphics and sung by stars wih immoral lifestyles is not for Christians. Then the authors have this to say:

"Rock music, though only one of many influences, has often been the deciding factor that pushes someone over the brink to choose suicide."[1]

Whether or not we accept the belief that backward masking registers in our mind and affects our future behavior, it is interesting to note that "subliminals are now being proven to affect the behavior of an individual, especially one who is emotionally involved in the message."[2] "We must agree that listening repeatedly to records promoting values which we detest does basically the same thing. Whether the messages are hidden or not, they *do* stay with us."[3]

"If you are filling your eyes and ears with garbage, you'll want more garbage. But if you are concentrating on good, healthy, upbuilding sights and sounds, you'll want all the more, and the result will be inner growth, rather than corruption. The decision is a personal one, however. The world provides more than enough ways to tempt your eyes and ears. It takes conscious, personal effort to avoid these potentially harmful influences."[4]

If these statements from experts on the subject really bothered you, you most likely have problems in the area of what you

---

[1]Dan and Steve Peters, *Why Knock Rock?* (Minneapolis: Bethany House Publishers, 1984), p. 155.

[2]Dan Peters and Steve Peters, *Rock's Hidden Persuader: The Truth About Backmasking* (Minneapolis: Bethany House Publishers, 1985), p. 114.

[3]*Why Knock Rock?*, p. 175.

[4]Ibid., p. 150.

hear and see. The big question is:

WHAT DO YOU PLAN TO DO ABOUT IT?

Which artists should you stop listening to? _____

_____

Which TV programs and movies should you stop watching?

_____

Are you willing to destroy videos, cassettes, or CDs? _____
Then do it *now!*

Are you willing to stop watching the movies and TV programs that are bad for you? _____

☑ Ask Yourself: Is This the Best Use of My Time, Money, Energy, and Influence?

It's pretty easy to see that it's better to listen to a song that honors God and goodness than to one that has lyrics about committing suicide or having one love affair after another. Getting involved in sports would benefit you more than boob-tubing it for hours every day. Being part of a Christian music group would beat spending summer vacation sleeping in every day until noon.

Other factors are involved in making excellent choices. Not everybody has the money to buy all that's necessary to collect stamps, go skiing, make model airplanes, take up sailing or scuba diving, and sign up for courses in oil painting or tennis. So it's a good idea to decide what activity would be your best recreational choice and then strive for excellence in it. If the guys on the hockey team are infamous party animals and the coach of the basketball team is a Christian, then choosing the sport where you find the better atmosphere is wise. If your best Christian friend is really into hiking, why not check it out even if you enjoy chess more? Investing in a stronger relationship with another Christian is time well spent. Don't just ooze into the empty spaces in your time schedule; *plan* to use your leisure time to the best advantage.

Colossians 3:17 tells us: "And whatever you do, whether in word or deed, do it all in the name of the Lord Jesus, giving thanks to God the Father through him." And 1 Corinthians 10:31, 32 tells us: "So whether you eat or drink or whatever you do, do it all for the glory of God. Do not cause anyone to stumble, whether Jews or Greeks or the church of God."

Instead of getting hung up on the "no-nos," take the positive approach. Use spare time to form some strong Christian friendships. Remember that there are tons of fun things you can do that will glorify God. Keep your body, which is the temple of the Holy Spirit, in good physical condition. Express the creativity God has placed within you. Get to know non-Christians through recreational activities so you can witness to them. All of this will result in a life that's pleasing to God. Becoming an expert on the Civil War, fixing cars, diving techniques, making the best cakes, or knowing a few magic tricks and some good clean jokes can give you self-confidence and help you fit into the group.

Prayerfully plan your recreational activities. Why not listen to music that will bring you closer to God? Why not design some original get-well cards for kids in the hospital or you're-being-thought-of cards for some older people in your community? You could teach a younger kid how to work the computer and influence him or her for Christ. A good day of skiing, or some other favorite pastime, could make you much more relaxed and ready for a hard week at school. Don't be a carbon-copy teen who just has to do what everyone else does.

Make excellent choices in the use of your leisure time that will leave you better off spiritually, emotionally, and physically.

☑ Setting Your Goal

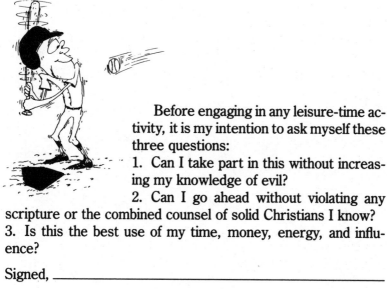

Before engaging in any leisure-time activity, it is my intention to ask myself these three questions:

1. Can I take part in this without increasing my knowledge of evil?

2. Can I go ahead without violating any scripture or the combined counsel of solid Christians I know?

3. Is this the best use of my time, money, energy, and influence?

Signed, _____

Things I know I must stop doing, and steps I plan to take:

_____

_____

_____

Signed, _____

Things I know I must stop reading, seeing, or listening to, and steps I plan to take: _____

_____

_____

_____

Signed, _____

4

Turning the Other Cheek and Other Impossible Goals

Learn to Love the Word Impossible

Some of the things Scripture tells us to do seem absolutely impossible—like Jesus' command to "turn the other cheek" when someone slaps you. The only thing that can turn those impossible goals into automatic reactions is the power of God. Jeremiah, speaking for the Lord, gave us an unchanging truth: "I am the Lord, the God of all mankind. Is anything too hard for me?" (Jeremiah 32:26). The truth is, you and I were created like automobiles, who cannot function smoothly without the supernatural energy of the Holy Spirit in our tanks. If you can be convinced of the superiority of "heavenly gasoline," you just might change brands.

✔️ Defining the Problem

"Derek's got brains to burn, but he's also got a chip on his shoulder."

"Jill's beautiful, but no one can get close to her."

"Rod is mad at the world, and I'd avoid him if I were you."

"Alicia is easily hurt, so watch what you say."

The list of ingrained behaviors could go on and on. If you haven't had an opportunity to become bitter at life, you can be sure you'll be presented with more than one chance. The devil will see to that. Eventually, someone will reject your best intentions, treat you unfairly, or take advantage of you. Difficult circumstances and seemingly impossible situations will face you.

Maybe you've already hit these "potholes in the road of life." Your parents may be so emotionally damaged that they think only of themselves. You may be a victim of your parents' divorce, rejection, substance abuse, or worse. Maybe you've never been accepted by your peers. Your best may never have been good enough to win you any special attention. Perhaps you feel lonely and forgotten, or your family's finances always limit you. Maybe you were forced to move away from all your friends. You might have a handicap or health problem, or feel painfully insecure and shy. Maybe you have an addiction that makes life unbearable.

Whenever you feel cheated by people or circumstances, you can easily catch a spiritual disease called *bitterness*. Its symptoms are: depression, self-pity, jealousy, and belittling others to make yourself feel better. If not treated, this disease of the soul can lead to more serious complications.

Or you can go to "Doctor" Jesus, who will prescribe that you learn about love, forgiveness, living at peace with everyone, and getting involved in the difficult process of rebuilding damaged relationships.

☛ Bitterness: The Root That Becomes a Tree

Resentment sets in motion a whole chain of events. With God's help you can confront resentment and wipe it out before it becomes a monster.

First, bitterness almost always begins with a feeling of hurt and rejection. A very sensitive person can feel overlooked when there is no good reason for feeling that way, but most often a real injustice starts the process.

Second, we were made to give and receive love. When that blueprint isn't followed, injury results. Trying to pretend you're so tough that nothing affects you never works. Both physical and emotional pain are signals that something is wrong. Ignoring the hurt can force it down into your subconscious, but that will not make it go away. In order to keep the still-open wound from being touched or bumped, the hurt person then develops unhealthy protective patterns. Here are a few of those patterns:

Revenge

Getting back in either an unconscious or premeditated way is designed to keep people from inflicting any more damage. While the don't-get-mad-get-even formula doesn't win any popularity contests, it does make people think twice before attacking you.

Keeping your distance

Creating emotional space just to make sure that no one gets too close to you is another way to keep from getting hurt again. Emotional space is created when you develop an attitude of superiority, becoming a loner, changing friends whenever a relationship demands something, or refusing to open up to anyone.

Perpetual pity party

Trying to get sympathy by becoming a walking talking rerun of the stories of your deprived childhood, broken romance, or of the unjust teacher or boss also serves as a warning that whoever wrongs you will get a lot of bad publicity.

Constant criticism

Putting down the other person before he or she has a chance to find fault with you keeps the mouth in motion. However, this best-defense-is-a-good-offense formula creates a lot of other problems for its users.

People pleasing

Trying to make everyone happy all the time so that no one would think of doing you any harm is very stressful. And when it fails, you can become very depressed.

All these warped responses can result when you do not choose to let God's supernatural power heal your hurt. Whether the wound is recent or one that's been festering for years, there are steps to freedom. You can make excellent choices that will keep you from becoming a bitter person whom no one wants to be around, someone whose physical and emotional health has been wrecked by unforgiveness. *Unless Jesus lives within you and you are plugged in to His power, however, these steps will not work for you.*

☑ The Road to *It-Doesn't-Hurt-Anymore*

Willingness to forgive

Because Jesus forgave you and offers you His superhuman ability to pardon the thoughtless and unkind actions of others, you can forgive—no matter how horrible the offense.

Forgiving does not *mean*

- that what the other person did to you was okay. It might have been rotten, terrible, and sinful.
- that you won't face a lot of *emotional* turmoil because of the situation.

Forgiving does *mean*

- that you are *willing* to forgive. This means that every time your emotions kick up a storm over the issue, you can sincerely say, "I forgive _____ for what they did."
- that you pray for the person who hurt you, and honestly desire God's best for his or her life.
- that you intend to love that person by faith—that you're willing to depend on God to fill the "kindness molds" you make with His genuine love—going out of your way to help the person, buying them a little gift, being friendly although they won't speak to you.

Receive God's Healing for Your Emotional Wounds

Ask Jesus to treat the injury.

Instead of trying to act tough, ask the Lord to heal the hurt you felt when you weren't invited to go on the camping trip, when your father said you were good-for-nothing, or when the guy or gal you liked started dating someone else. Each time the pain comes back, pray again that Jesus will cure your aching heart.

Take a strong dose of the sovereignty of God.

In case the term is unfamiliar, "the sovereignty of God" is a theological way of saying that God is completely in charge of the universe. He not only runs the show, He's looking out for you too! As Paul says, "And we know that in all things God works for the good of those who love him, who have been called according to his purpose" (Romans 8:28). That's a wonderful promise to remember.

In practical terms, this means that if you've surrendered

your life to God and are willing to obey and follow Him, He'll make sure that nothing can touch your life that will not ultimately turn out for your good.

It operates like this. Let's say someone has stolen your girlfriend or boyfriend, and right now you have a broken heart. When you submit these events to God, you can trust that He has someone much better for you in your future. Your father's alcoholism might be messing up your family now, but God will use the victory He'll give you in the middle of these hard experiences, perhaps so that you can help many children and teens in similar situations. Or if you have a physical handicap, God will turn your suffering into a testimony of His grace, which will convince many people of their need of Christ. God has a good plan for bad situations.

In order to encourage your faith, memorize Psalm 57:2: "I cry out to God Most High, to God, who fulfills his purpose for me." And also Philippians 1:6: "Being confident of this, that he who began a good work in you will carry it on to completion until the day of Christ Jesus." God gives His guarantee that nothing anyone can do can ruin your life—unless you let it. The fact that God's plan for you cannot be derailed by some cruel person is of great comfort when you are misunderstood or betrayed.

Another step in recovering from inner wounds is to talk things over with a trusted Christian friend. Expressing the problem in words to a sympathetic listener is good therapy. Besides, you're probably so emotionally involved in the situation that you can't think objectively. The advice of a mature Christian can be invaluable.

Finally, get so caught up in serving Jesus that you take your mind off the pain.

This step can never replace any of the first three steps. Some people quickly overdose on Christian work because their ulterior motive is to cover the guilt of an unforgiving spirit or refusing to admit that they've been badly hurt.

But once you have forgiven the person who did the damage and opened your heart for healing, give yourself completely to the greatest cause on earth—that of increasing the population of heaven and discipling the people whose lives God is dramatically changing. You'll have little time to remember injustices, harsh words, and traumatic experiences.

In order to find freedom from bitterness, you must first settle old accounts with forgiveness and God's love-your-enemies kind of love. You need to hook up with the "Jesus Power and Light Company," and take advantage of His healing offer. Recognize that each time someone mistreats you, or makes fun of you, or rejects you, then you have a marvelous opportunity to pray down some miracles. Ask God for the supernatural ability to pardon the culprit and genuinely care about him or her. Let Jesus put His bandages on your wound. Review the promises that assure you that God is calling the shots, and discuss the matter with your pastor or a good Christian friend. Finally, serve God with more enthusiasm than ever. The scenery on the road to It-Doesn't-Hurt-Anymore is very refreshing.

☑ Setting Your Goal

I will take seriously the promises of Scripture, including: "But if you do not forgive men their sins, your Father will not forgive your sins" (Matthew 6:15); and "I can do everything through him who gives me strength" (Philippians 4:13). I determine to immediately forgive each person who hurts me—no matter how unfair it is, no matter how much it will cost me, and even if the problem is caused by a sinning Christian who should know better. Although my emotions may not follow right away, it is my will to forgive.

People I have not really forgiven, but will forgive now. _____

_____

_____

Signed, _____

Hurts I'm carrying, which I now ask Jesus to heal. _____

_____

_____

_____

Signed, _____

5
You and Your Mirror

Dressing the Part

Although you can't decide whether you want to be tall or short, how big your feet will be, or how long your nose is, you *do* make a lot of choices that affect your physical appearance. The hairstyle you select, the quantity of money you spend on clothes, the amount of time you spend in front of the mirror—all reflect your deeper values.

Clothes do not make the man or woman. But it's surprising what you can learn about people just by noticing how they dress. What you wear—or don't wear—sends some interesting messages. The girl in the super-tight, super-short skirt obviously wants guys to be physically attracted to her. The gal with dirty uncombed hair, slouching around in an oversized man's shirt and baggy sweat pants is really saying, "I don't care very much." The guy who copies a famous rock star is signaling his approval of a certain kind of music or lifestyle. The super-jock who dresses the part is making a statement about how much he prizes his physical body.

How you look *is* important. So it's not surprising that the Bible gives us some dress-code suggestions. Some Christians have taken the *New Testament* guidelines as rock-hard standards for all time. Most believers feel they are directions given during a certain age, based on the significance of each practice at the time. Many feel we can draw general principles from these examples, but that we should not become legalistic and judge others by what they wear or how they look. This view, in my opinion, makes more biblical sense.

Let's examine a case in point. Paul tells us:

> Now I want you to realize that the head of every man is Christ, and the head of the woman is man, and the head of Christ is God. Every man who prays or prophesies with his head covered dishonors his head. And every woman who prays or prophesies with her head uncovered dishonors her head—it is just as though her head were shaved. (1 Corinthians 11:3)

Interpreting the passage in context, it is clear that the man would dishonor his head—Christ—by not observing the Greek and Roman custom for men to worship bareheaded. This reflects *local* custom, however, because Hebrew men, like Orthodox Jews today, prayed with their heads covered. It seems illogical that Paul would tell the men to observe the Corinthian way of showing proper respect and next lay down a hard and fast rule that women must observe for all time.

Following the information provided by verse 3, the "head" that the woman would dishonor would be her husband—and possibly for unmarried girls, a future spouse. Throughout the known world at that time all women covered their heads when they appeared in public, except for street prostitutes who advertised by taking off the traditional veil. Furthermore, the punishment for adultery was shaving the head of the woman. For this reason it was a shame for a woman to have her hair shaved or cut off. Long hair and a head covering symbolized modesty, chastity, and purity in Corinth in the first century A.D. A Christian woman would ruin not only her own testimony but the reputation of the congregation by praying or prophesying in public meetings with her head uncovered. Paul wanted Christian women to visually demonstrate their moral values by keeping their hair long and their heads covered. The teaching of First Corinthians 11 can be boiled down to a few practical principles:

The Dress or Appearance of a Christian Should Never Bring Shame or Ridicule Upon the Cause of Christ

This could include wearing clothes from the last century, or causing your neighbor to comment, "I wouldn't let my daughter out of the house with jeans as tight as hers—and *she* claims to be a Christian," or to run around with that I-just-got-out-of-bed-and-I-slept-in-my-clothes look, or wearing T-shirts with questionable messages. Any one of these things could mean that you are not living up to the spiritual principle set out in Scripture.

A Christian should avoid the things that immediately turn people off since ambassadors for Christ should not needlessly offend. The girl who globs on a clown's amount of makeup and enough jewelry to start a small store may be a sincere Christian, but she will have a hard time because of her appearance, like it or not. The guy who sports the most extreme new hairstyle will be accused of only wanting to draw attention to himself. Clothes considered outlandish by the majority don't help you win friends and influence people.

God wants you to look your best and make a good impression for Him. And He'll help you! Sincerely pray about what hairstyle you should choose, what clothes you should buy, and what jewelry would be appropriate. God can give you some great ideas you never thought of. You are the temple of the Holy Spirit. Ask God if His temple is decorated in conformity with His taste. If not, be willing to change.

Scripture also teaches: "I also want women to dress modestly, with decency and propriety, not with braided hair or gold or pearls or expensive clothes, but with good deeds, appropriate for women who profess to worship God" (1 Timothy 2:9, 10). Peter, speaking to wives, said, "Your beauty should not come from outward adornment, such as braided hair and the wearing of gold jewelry and fine clothes. Instead, it should be that of your inner self, the unfading beauty of a gentle and quiet spirit, which is of great worth in God's sight" (1 Peter 3:3–4).

In ancient times, men had fewer choices to make about their appearance than they do today. For this reason and the fact that women are generally more concerned about dress, ornaments, and hairstyles than men, these passages are directed to females. From them, however, we can draw principles that apply to both sexes.

☛ The Christian Should Always Dress Modestly

It is true that "dressing modestly" meant something different at the time of Queen Victoria than it means today. Even so, a Christian must not just give in to every style and trend without evaluating it in terms of modesty. If the latest fad is wearing tight tops and shorts that are super-sexy, the Christian must resist the temptation to follow everyone else. Buying a bathing suit these days requires some thought and prayer—and a lot of shopping.

Because guys receive sexual stimulation from what they see—and God made them like that—the Christian girl must dress responsibly. Sometimes girls don't realize that what they're wearing is causing the guys around them to battle unclean thoughts. There are good reasons for dressing to prevent mind pollution.

Jesus said, "Things that cause people to sin are bound to come, but woe to that person through whom they come" (Luke 17:1). He also taught, "Anyone who looks at a woman lustfully has already committed adultery with her in his heart" (Matthew 5:28).

Wearing a bikini to the beach, putting on a pair of pants that fit like a coat of paint, or slipping into a revealing blouse could cause some heavy-duty damage. If you feel convicted of wearing clothes that have been a stumbling block to someone, you should ask God for forgiveness and change your habits of dress.

A girl who had recently committed her life to Christ expressed the secret worry of many: "If I dress like a Christian, not one guy will notice me." She's right—*some* won't! But if all a guy is looking for is the best body, you'll lose him anyway as soon as something better comes along. Many women who lured their husbands by dressing provocatively wonder why they later lose their men to younger women. Any relationship based primarily on sexual attraction is doomed to failure. So you're really not missing out on much. Besides, you need to learn to trust God to bring the right guy into your life instead of making every day a "fishing expedition."

Christian guys need to avoid the world's mentality of not looking beyond the obvious. The gorgeous girl who struts her stuff has been the downfall of many a young Christian man. Girls whose goal is to marry a man of God will find that guys who are really following God appreciate modest attire. It's possible to be extremely attractive without compromising on modesty. How about turning your creative talents in that direction?

Open communication between men and women on this matter can be extremely helpful. A girl should pay utmost attention to what her father or brothers think of her clothes—and even ask for their opinion. Guys who find that the way the girls in their churches are dressing tempts them in their thought life should talk it over with their pastors. In some youth groups, guys fill out anonymous questionnaires rating the latest fads in girls' clothes on a scale of provocativeness, and the girls get to see the results. It's entirely in line for a guy to say to his girlfriend, "I wish you wouldn't wear your skirts so short and your blouses so tight—the way you dress tempts me."

One day when I was reading a book on Roman history, I discovered something interesting. Many wealthy women of that time had a special slave just to fix their hair. The intricate braiding, which was the "high fashion do," took about four hours to complete! Often, gold and pearl ornaments were placed in the hair. Copying this style was extremely expensive and very time consuming. I don't think that either Peter or Paul felt it was a sin to braid your hair, and I don't believe they are saying that wearing jewelry is wrong. In my opinion they were laying down a principle:

✔ A Christian Who Cares About Spiritual, Eternal Goals Will Not Spend Too Much Time and Money on Outward Appearance

If you're addicted to your mirror, if the appearance of a *zit* is a major catastrophe, if you just have to have the most expensive and stylish clothes, you have a problem in this area. Although you may never have thought of it this way, having to look "just so" all the time is a form of spiritual slavery. For example, psychologists have discovered that some girls feel like a zero if they're not wearing all their makeup. Therapists are advising that the patient go one day a week without any makeup, just to stop depending on it for a feeling of worth. If you've fallen for the everybody-notices-everything-about-me-and-I-must-look-perfect-all-the-time deception, it's time to get free.

For all the talk of independence and freedom, millions of teens let a few designers—who are out to get their bucks!—tell them exactly how to dress. Advertisers have done a number on you if your athletic shoes must be the most expensive, or if you must buy a costly cream to have a flawless complexion, or if you urgently need the latest diet-exercise plan to achieve a Hollywood physique. What you wear and how you appear to others does *not* determine who you are.

Jesus loved you so much He died for you, and that makes you incredibly valuable and worthwhile—no matter what. You can dare to break out of the mold. You don't have to feel like a loser if you don't have enough money to buy Air Jordans or a new "Watchman" to hang on your belt.

You can wear more on the beach than those around you. You can choose styles that reflect modest good taste, and reject the ones that don't.

Fashion is important in every society, and it's even mentioned in the Law of Moses: "A woman must not wear men's clothing, nor a man wear women's clothing, for the Lord your God detests anyone who does this" (Deuteronomy 22:5).

Since what is considered "men's clothing" or "women's clothing" has varied over the centuries, depending on location and culture, it's pretty difficult to apply this verse to any specific type of clothing. In fact, the robes worn by men and women when this law was given were similar.

There is a spiritual principle that stands, though: One of Satan's strategies is to try to erase sexual differences by getting men and women to exchange roles and clothes. In order to worship the goddess for whom the Israelites disobediently erected Asherah poles, women donned armor and the men put on women's clothing. Today, you can see this kind of perversion in the transvestite. Therefore, girls should guard against that masculine look, and guys should avoid anything decidedly feminine, if their intent is to identify more with the opposite gender than their own.

An addiction to fine and expensive clothes can trap just about anyone. In the inner city, kids have been brutally attacked just because someone wanted their top brand athletic shoes or sharp-looking jacket. It's more and more common for people to shoplift in order to support the habit of having to have the best, even though they can't afford it. There are Christians who habitually spend all their tithe money on the latest fashions. The Bible warns you against getting hooked on fine clothes.

A famous Christian woman of a past generation had three rules for her clothes—each item had to be practical, reasonably priced, and in style. Avoiding extremes is always a good idea. Although God wants you well-dressed, He says to you, "Do not store up for yourselves treasures on earth [and most young people have a pretty big part of their treasure in the clothes closet], where moth and rust destroy, and where thieves break in and steal. But store up for yourselves treasures in heaven . . . for where your treasure is, there your heart will be also" (Matthew 6:19–21).

You'd do well to concentrate more on gentleness and goodness than on outward appearance. The joy and peace of Jesus do more to improve one's looks than any beauty treatment or a super-close shaver. A great smile that comes from a heart at peace with God is a terrific asset. The strength of a man who faithfully serves God is incredibly attractive. The tenderness of a woman who brings the comfort of Christ into difficult situations is irresistible. God invites you to live on a higher plain.

Jesus explains this new lifestyle:

> Don't worry about . . . what you will wear. Is not . . . the body more important than clothes? . . . Why worry about clothes? See how the lilies of the field grow. They do not labor or spin. Yet I tell you that not even Solomon in all his splendor was dressed like one of these. If that is how God clothes the grass of the field, which is here today and tomorrow is thrown into the fire, will he not much more clothe you, O you of little faith? So do not worry, saying . . . "What shall we wear?" . . . But seek first his kingdom and his righteousness, and all these things will be given you as well. (Matthew 6:25–33)

✔ Setting Your Goal

Check the areas where you feel you need to change:

- ☐ I agree to spend less time in front of the mirror.
- ☐ I agree to pay more attention to my appearance.
- ☐ I agree to pay less attention to my appearance.
- ☐ I agree to wear clothes that are less provocative.
- ☐ I admit that I'm addicted to always having to have the sharpest, most expensive clothes. I'm willing to change.
- ☐ I admit that my hairstyle/jewelry/clothing send some wrong messages, and I'm willing to change.

Lord, by your grace and with your help it is my sincere intention to do the following things so my appearance and my attitudes will be more pleasing to you. _____

_____

_____

_____

_____

_____

Signed, _____

6
Have You Signed the Declaration of Independence?

Give Me Liberty—Complete With Instruction Manual

After being lectured by your mother for not cleaning your room—or after having your plans to play volleyball canceled by a punishment math assignment—or after receiving a ticket for going 40 miles an hour in a 30-mile-an-hour zone, you're probably ready to search for the Paradise of Freedom Unlimited. Just doing what you want to do and getting everyone off your back does appear attractive—if you don't know all the facts of life. Ignorance about the scriptural principles for living under God-ordained authority has resulted in so many if-I-only-had-it-to-do-over-again choices. But your life can be different *if* you learn the system and how to live happily with it.

The transition from childhood to adulthood means rethinking your concept of authority. The scheme of things seen through a child's eyes tends to produce the following attitudes: My parents are right. The teacher said so, and that settles it. The policeman is my friend. I should be "good," and "good" is defined by the "big people" around me. That world view is shaken by a teenage awareness that parents can have some pretty big character flaws, that teachers don't always know what they're talking about, that the boss might not be playing fair and that government has gigantic problems. Confused and unable to cope with this new perception, a lot of young people become "rebellious." The whole teen culture seems to reinforce making fun of adults who just aren't with it, pointing out the inconsistencies in authority figures, and creating a youth-centered "new world order" that rejects all the taboos of the past.

Before you put your John Hancock on this new "Declaration of Independence," there are some important things to consider.

God did not create you to be a mindless, spineless creature bossed around by some autocratic authority—nor does He want you to be controlled by the rebellious rampage set in motion by a certain segment of society. God thought that your right to make your own decisions is so important that He created you with a free will—a will so free, in fact, that you can even reject your Maker if you choose. God won't *force* you to do anything: Your independence is top priority with Him. However, He built into the universe rewards for using freedom correctly and punishments for abusing it. He also laid down principles for the successful use of our liberties.

If you want to flow with the current of God's creation, it requires voluntary submission to authority. Deciding to ignore or go against your parents, teachers, bosses, or government has serious consequences—repercusions you should be smart enough to avoid. Disobedience to parents ignites conflict and causes stress. Rebellion at school introduces you to all kinds of disciplinary measure. Workers who can't go by the rules miss out on promotions or get fired. Being on the wrong side of the law can land you in a concrete cell. Having worked with young people for years, I can make this observation: Rebellious young people are very unhappy. *I have never seen an exception.*

God created the universe and He made up the system. He made you free to choose His way. Of course, you can reject the instructions given in His How Human Beings Function Best manual, but it's a decision you'll live to regret. It would be a lot smarter to understand God's reasoning and to learn the ropes. Living God's way means learning to see *all things* under God's loving control, so that loving your enemy and submitting to authority become normal responses. You will need the power of the Holy Spirit to make this switch. It's good to know that God offers a never-ending supply of His superhuman strength to react to situations His way.

☑ Adopting God's Objectives

Our goals are usually based on motives like these: *This will make me happy. It's more convenient. It's less work. It's what I want to do. It's what everyone else is doing. This will make people notice and respect me. It's the road to popularity. This is a good way to make more money. It will make me more attractive to members of the opposite sex.* And you could probably make some additions to this list.

God has two purposes, however, that far outweigh all others:

1. He loves you so much that He wants you to spend eternity with Him—"not wanting anyone to perish, but everyone to come to repentance" (2 Peter 3:9). From God's point of view, allowing tough circumstances and difficult people to enter your life is worth it if it causes you to realize your need of a Savior. Eternity without Him is so terrible that He will go to any lengths to try to wake you up to the need of accepting His way of salvation.

2. Once you become a born-again Christian, God wants to transform your personality and make it like His own. "For those God foreknew he also predestined to be conformed to the likeness of his Son" (Romans 8:29). If a diamond could feel, it would not enjoy all the chipping and polishing that's necessary to bring out its hidden brilliance. Like a diamond, you may have to suffer as God works on your personality. But reflecting Jesus to a world hungry for love and meaning is so important, God will let you go through a lot of hard experiences to achieve that end.

One reason there is so much rebellion in the world today is that most people have rejected God's purposes in exchange for momentary pleasures. According to today's thinking, anything that interferes with comfort, fun, economic well-being, or instant gratification is bad. The world says it is your "right" to experience pleasure and a life free of rules. This is a foolish illusion.

God's way is different. It means freedom within boundaries that will keep you safe, submission to someone who will lift you up and give you dignity, and obedience with joy. The ability to live this way only comes when the dynamic energy of the Holy Spirit is present—a catalyst from outer space! If you're willing to depend on God, and to live by His principles, you can make some excellent choices regarding the use of your personal liberty.

☑ Submission to Authority Is Part of God's Overall Plan

> Honor your father and your mother, so that you may live long in the land the Lord your God is giving you. (Exodus 20:12)
>
> He who obeys instructions guards his soul, but he who is contemptuous of his ways will die. (Proverbs 19:16)
>
> Obey your leaders and submit to their authority. (Hebrews 13:17)
>
> Everyone must submit himself to the governing authorities, for there is no authority except that which God has established. The authorities that exist have been established by God. (Romans 13:1)

Obedience to those the Lord has placed over you *is* God's will for you—not because adults are always right, not because the leaders always know more than you do, not because the badge of authority makes a superior person, but because a spirit of submissiveness, cooperation, and love makes you more like Jesus, and because God uses those in authority to protect you.

Proving you're right is not important: Being right with God is. Obeying your parents even while missing Tim's birthday party to go to the airport to meet Aunt Helen seems like the end of the world now but will build in you unselfish character. Refusing to complain about the ridiculous assignment given by the flustered, inexperienced teacher is a way of showing her respect and compassion. Not reminding your youth pastor that you told him no one would be interested in coming to a "Sing-Along" demonstrates your submissiveness and willingness to cooperate. Receiving the love of Jesus and passing it along when others would demand their rights and expose the errors made by those in authority is a tremendous evidence of God's work in your life.

God does use your parents and other adult leaders to give you sound advice and prevent you from making costly mistakes. Teachers can offer constructive criticism that can be extremely valuable. Bible teachers can give you the needed guidance to line your life up with God's will. Choosing not to rebel against authority yields big dividends.

☑ God's Appeals-Court System

What if your parents really blow it? What if your idea is better than the leader's? What if the teacher is unfair? What if you're asked to do something wrong? You have two extremely powerful weapons: You can pray, and you can appeal to authority. To maintain balance in the authority-submission arena, you must learn to use both of them effectively. Some teenagers conform outwardly but inside they're building up for an explosion because they have never learned to correctly express their views to those in charge. They don't know how powerful a well-presented request can be. Others use the he-won't-listen-anyway excuse for bypassing the process of appeal and heading down the road to rebellion. Few bother to pray for those in authority over them.

Prayer can prevent *and* resolve problems. Daily, ask God to give your parents wisdom and to make wise decisions. Raising you may be harder than you think! Pray for your principal, your teachers, your boss, your church leaders, and your government authorities. Pray that God will show you how to relate to each one—especially for those you clash with! Some problems can be solved by prayer alone. The God who could arrange all the circumstances so that the stubborn, hard-hearted pharaoh would change his mind can certainly work on your father's attitudes. Remember, "the king's heart is in the hand of the Lord; he directs it like a watercourse wherever he pleases" (Proverbs 21:1).

Most leaders will listen if you learn how to make requests based on God's principles, which include showing respect.

☞ Learning a Thing or Two From Queen Esther

Queen Esther was married to a man who drank too much and who was unpredictable and ruthless. Because he was king, he answered to no one. Once an elderly man approached him and offered to give money for the upcoming military campaign if only his son could be exempt from serving in the army. King Ahasuerus commanded that the son be brought to him. Before the eyes of the horrified father the boy was cut in two, the halves separated, and the army ordered to march between them. And this was the guy Queen Esther had to face when she wanted to make her request! Her success proves that an appeal made in the right way can be unbelievably powerful.

The following steps include the biblical principles you can follow when you try to get someone in authority to change their mind:

Specifically pray for God's wisdom in handling the situation. Check your standing with God and with human authorities.

Better yet, prepare for this moment way in advance by living a life that is pleasing to God and showing genuine submissiveness and respect for those over you. Once I listened to a tearful girl tell me her biology teacher falsely accused her of cheating the first time she really studied and earned a decent grade. When she told him the truth, he wouldn't listen to her. She admitted she'd cheated on other exams and lied when confronted. That teacher had no reason to believe her. She'd already ruined the relationship, and she had no basis to make a strong, effective appeal.

Unless you repent of pride, rebellion, laziness, a bad attitude, disobedience, and other sins against God or human authorities, your request won't do much good.

Avoid appeals that are designed just to help you get your own way or to enable you to escape consequences you deserve.

When you shout and accuse parents of being cruel so you can wear them down and get the car, or force them to raise your allowance, you are out of line. This behavior has no place in the life of a Christian. And if you've done something wrong, take the punishment you have coming *without* trying to get off easy.

Save your appeals for situations that involve injustice, for times when the authority doesn't understand all the facts, and when a wrong decision could produce some big problems. If your appeal upholds God's standards, He will be interested in helping you present your case.

Wait until the right time to make your request.

Pray the problem through so that you'll be at peace *no matter what the answer is.* Don't make your plea while you're still upset. Be sure to approach the other person when he or she is calm and has the time to really listen to you. Showing your willingness to sacrifice will convince the man or woman in authority of your sincerity and may help get the results you're after. For example, it is much better to offer to report on two other books to replace the questionable one you've been asked to read than to demand that you be excused from having to do the assignment.

Give accurate information.

Exaggerations like "Everybody else has one," or "You're the only teacher in the world who gives this much homework" are not only detrimental to your plea, they're lies. Be sure you stick strictly to the truth. Your petition needs to be supported by facts, so be sure that you gather your information carefully and do all your homework. Remember that God is able to bless honesty and diligence.

Maintain the right attitudes.

These attitudes will get you a *no* response: arrogance ("I want it—*now!*"); irritation ("Come on. You can lend me just a little more extra money,") and snippiness ("You're on the phone all the time. Why can't I talk just five minutes more?").

More appeals are probably turned down because of bad attitudes than because of any other reason. If you show your loyalty, respect, and willingness to obey *regardless of the response,* parents, teachers, coaches, and other leaders are much more likely to grant your request. Why? Because they can sense that you will obey them when they need you to.

Use the right words.

Pleasing words flow naturally from a heart motivated by love and service. Proverbs 22:11 tells us, "He who loves a pure heart and whose speech is gracious will have the king for his friend"— as well as his principal, his teachers, and his supervisors at work!

Correct attitudes are most important. But it is also wise to think through your explanation thoroughly. Be sure your point is clear. Are there any objections to your plan of action? Decide ahead of time how you will answer them.

Display a right response even if your appeal is rejected.

Remember that no person can stop the will of God. When Hudson Taylor asked for the hand of his girlfriend, Maria, in marriage, her guardian said no. But as the two patiently waited and prayed, her uncle decided to overrule the decision of the guardian. Realize that God can use even an unreasonable authority to make you into a diamond that shines. Graciously accept a *no* answer to your appeal. It might be good to plan what you'll say if your request is turned down.

☛ The Biblical Basis for Some Excellent Choices[1]

If you accept these biblical facts and decide to base your life on them, you'll save yourself all the trouble of rebelling!

1. Choose to . . . believe that God is in control of the universe.

Since authority is designed by Him, He will use the authorities in your life to draw you closer to himself and refine your character. *If you follow His principles,* He will protect you.

2. Choose to . . . become skillful in making appeals to authority.

Instead of simmering in angry silence or conforming outwardly and hating every minute of it, learn to bring important issues to the person in charge. Replace constant complaining and gossip with a petition directed to the right person. Replace sarcasm and rebellion with an ability to bring your requests to those in authority over you.

3. Choose to . . . obey God rather than man.

What if you're asked to do something against your conscience, which you can support from Scripture, and your appeal fails? Then be ready to take the consequences while still maintaining your attitude of cooperation and submission. Remember, "great is your reward in heaven" if you choose to get fired for refusing to lie to cover up for the boss.

---

[1]These steps are adapted from *The Key to Freedom Under Authority,* Institute in Basic Youth Conflicts, 1978.

✔️ Setting Your Goal

I will remember that the God who controls the universe will protect me, His child, from abuse by authorities. He will use my parents, my teachers, my boss, and my spiritual leaders to form in me the character of Christ. Keeping this in mind, I plan to keep a submissive attitude and correctly appeal to authorities when I feel I have a good basis for doing so. I will disobey only when asked to do things contrary to the Word of God.

Signed, _____

When I decide to appeal to authority, I plan to fill out the form on the following page before making my request.

Signed, _____

✏ 1. Appeal to Authority Form*

1. Have you prayed enough about the problem so that you're calm and willing to accept whatever answer is given? _____
2. Are you in right standing with God and the authority involved? _____ Are there any actions or attitudes you need to repent of? _____ If so, what are they? ____

_____

_____

3. Is this appeal just an excuse to get your own way? _____
If not, on what basis are you making the appeal? _____

_____

4. When would be the best time to make the request? _____
Why? _____

_____

5. Write down the facts: _____

_____

_____

_____

Write down any exaggeration you might be tempted to throw in—then decide you will not use it! _____

_____

_____

6. How can you show your loyalty and respect to authority while making the request? _____

_____

7. Write out exactly what you intend to say: _____

_____

_____

_____

_____

8. What objections do you expect? _____

_____

_____

How do you intend to answer them? _____

_____

_____

_____
*Make photocopies of the form so that you have them on hand when needed.

9. Write down the ready response you intend to give if your request is rejected: _____

_____

_____

_____

7
Reeboks, Credit Cards, and Eternal Investments

Your Money; Your Choice

Sara loves to shop. Whenever she goes to the mall, she finds several items she just *can't* live without. She charges just about everything—and always finds there's "too much *month* left at the end of the *money.*" Then she has to add overtime hours to her work schedule, so she's too tired to enjoy the few recreational activities she can squeeze in. And her grades are suffering big-time! Sara envies Mallory, who leads a girls' Bible study and is on the swim team. But it's never occurred to Sara that Mallory's lifestyle is possible only because she's chosen to live on a limited budget. . . .

Brad despises rich people, those who flaunt their possessions—and he hates work. His style is laid-back and casual, so he only needs a few pairs of old jeans, some shirts, a jacket, his guitar, and a small TV. He doesn't appreciate that his parents give him free room and board and a little spending money, which he stretches to the limit. He bums rides, and figures that if he doesn't happen to have any money, somebody else will always pick up the check.

If he doesn't return what he borrowed, it doesn't bother him much. And he can usually charm some girl into supplying him with whatever he forgot to bring to school. . . .

Ashly lives in an affluent neighborhood, and she's accustomed to having everything. Recently, her father was forced to drastically cut back on spending. Ashly is having trouble coping. Why? Because her self-acceptance is based on wearing the sharpest clothes in school. When she doesn't get constant compliments on stunning new outfits, and when her family had to drop their membership in the most exclusive athletic club, she felt as if she'd dropped a couple rungs down the social ladder. She can no longer buy new friends by inviting them to expensive places and giving them lavish gifts. In fact, several girls she used to hang around with have lost interest in her. Having the money to buy whatever she wanted was Ashly's security, so now she's worried about the future. What if her father's business were to fail altogether? Maybe no rich guys will want to date her. What if she has to get by on last year's wardrobe? What if she can't buy whatever she *wants*?

By setting scriptural financial goals and following biblical principles, you can avoid falling into any of these extremes. First Timothy 6:6–10 provides some clear teaching on the Christian and possessions:

> But godliness with contentment is great gain. For we brought nothing into the world, and we can take nothing out of it. But if we have food and clothing, we will be content with that. People who want to get rich fall into temptation and a trap and into many foolish and harmful desires that plunge men into ruin and destruction. For the love of money is a root of all kinds of evil. Some people, eager for money, have wandered from the faith and pierced themselves with many griefs.

Understand *God's* Purposes for Money and Possessions

1. Money and possessions supply God-designed basic needs and give us opportunities to express creativity and beauty.

The need for food, clothing, and shelter was built into God's universe. The Lord also created us with a capacity to appreciate color, style, design, and comfort. Any philosophy which teaches that we must completely deny the physical, material world in order to be "spiritual" is not biblically based. The Bible has a great deal to say about money, possessions, and working for our keep. It describes the beauty of Solomon's temple, gives the Passover menu, tells of a lesson Jeremiah learned from watching a potter, and relates details about the wall built around Jerusalem. Property, artwork, and financial resources are not bad in themselves. Nor is God automatically pleased with poverty, austerity, or great material sacrifice.

He is, however, terribly concerned with our attitudes toward material things. This is expressed in Deuteronomy 8:17, 18:

"You may say to yourself, 'My power and the strength of my hands have produced this wealth for me.' But remember the Lord your God, for it is he who gives you the ability to produce wealth." Putting trust in money instead of God is an all-too-common fiasco. God gives financial blessing, and He wants the recipient to maintain an attitude of thankfulness. Give God all the credit for your success, and use your material resources as *He* directs.

When Job realized that he'd lost all he had, he fell to the ground to worship God. This is what he said: "The Lord gave and the Lord has taken away; may the name of the Lord be praised." Because of all the questions he later had about suffering, we sometimes forget about the great attitude he had toward wealth. Even Satan realized that losing all his earthly goods couldn't make a dent in Job's faith.

In humility, realize that God has only lent you His money and possessions. This will keep you from a lot of harmful attitudes. Instead of trying to keep up with what "everyone else" owns, you can concentrate on contentment and gratitude. Complaining can be replaced by thanking God for each gift—a pepperoni pizza, an awesome new sweater, your beat-up bike, a TV that works, and even your biology book! Apologies for a small house, an old car, or less expensive clothes are completely unnecessary, because God in His sovereign wisdom has decided how much stuff to loan to you.

When you are secure in the knowledge that what you own doesn't determine your real worth, you can relax and enjoy what you *do* have. Competing with others to show up in the sharpest ski outfit, to own the coolest stereo, and to throw the most sensational party were not meant to be part of your life. It's time you learned the godliness-with-contentment-is-great-gain secret.

2. Money and possessions teach us to look to Him as our heavenly Father and supplier of all good things.

Part of the beauty of a good father-child relationship is the child's dependence on its father for all physical needs. A caring daddy wants to supply a new pair of shoes, a burger, or a bigger tricycle. When the child wants a drink, a great new toy, or a ride at the carnival, he just asks Daddy. Giving and receiving is part of that "special something" that builds ties between parents and children.

You and I are designed to be dependent on our heavenly Father because He wants a special relationship with each one of us. It should be totally natural for you to tell God that your winter boots leak and you don't have the money to buy new ones. When you get invited to go bowling after you've spent your last dime, prayer should be your first response. If your mom can't make the payments, ask God to come to the rescue. Your security should be in the God whose bank account is always in good shape.

If you start trusting the *gifts* instead of the *Giver,* you will live with stress and anxiety. Constantly afraid of losing what you have, you'll never be able to fully enjoy it. But if Jesus is the love of your life and you look to Him as the Source of everything you need, you'll experience a great deal of freedom. "Command those who are rich in this present world [and compared to the rest of the world, that most likely includes you] not to be arrogant nor to put their hope in wealth, which is so uncertain, but to put their hope in God, who richly provides us with everything for our enjoyment" (1 Timothy 6:17).

When you can't afford an item you really want, or when your favorite possession is damaged or stolen, or when you lose your job—you get an opportunity to discover where your confidence really is. Failing this type of exam indicates your need to repent of materialism, and your need to get better acquainted with the One who will "meet all your needs according to his glorious riches in Christ Jesus."

3. Money and possessions can become heavenly investments.

Money and material possessions are able to do some marvelous things. Five dollars of your money can buy a Bible, through which a person in another country can come to faith in God. The little gift you buy for your grandmother might just make her day. Offering to pay a friend's way to the youth retreat could cause him or her to stop straddling the fence and decide to follow Jesus completely. Helping the single mother in your church to buy medicine for her little girl could make you her special answer to prayer.

Christian radio programs reach Muslims for Christ. Missionaries translate Scripture into tribal languages. Orphanages give children a good home and solid Christian training. There are prison ministries, suicide hot lines, drug rehab centers, and those who bring the love of Jesus to victims of AIDS. *All of these endeavors cost money.* God's people have the opportunity of sharing in these great ventures through their financial giving.

In Old Testament times, the Israelites gave the first part of any crop as an offering to God, symbolizing that He deserved the best and had first priority in their lives. The tithe has the same purpose. We give God a tenth of all we earn, off the top, showing that He's more important to us than anybody else. Actually, the cheerful giving of our money is one of the few things we can do to demonstrate our love to God. Yet, as someone has explained, "God is nobody's debtor." When we give to Him, He returns the favor. " 'Bring the whole tithe into the storehouse, that there may be food in my house. Test me in this,' says the Lord Almighty, 'and see if I will not throw open the floodgates of heaven and pour out so much blessing that you will not have room enough for it' " (Malachi 3:10). Besides that, it's a great feeling to use your money—which represents a big chunk of your time and energy—to help win the world for Jesus.

Start now. Tithe. Give God a tenth of all you make—your earnings or your allowance. Invest extra money in God's kingdom and the dividends will be tremendous. If you live to give, you can expect a lot of exciting things to happen.

4. Money and possessions can help members of the body of Christ learn to depend on each other.

Have you ever wondered why God didn't just give every Christian in the world an equal amount of financial assets? God arranged a system in which diligence and hard work are rewarded—but more than that, He has another purpose for money: It is a means by which we can bless other Christians and receive love and care from them.

It was such a little thing but it was a real faith-builder. A friend of mine had done me a favor and I decided to show my thankfulness with a gift of money. I wrote a check for the amount I felt impressed by God to give, and sent it off with my thank-you note. Days later, she called to tell me it was the *exact* amount needed to buy an item she'd prayed for. Needless to say, it made us both excited about the God who supplies all our needs!

If your financial resources are severely limited, be willing to let God use other Christians to help you out. Instead of complaining or unfavorably comparing yourself to others, *pray, and watch God work*. If you have more than you need (and most likely you do, a lot more), God can use you to sponsor a child in the Philippines, to buy new shoes for the kid at school who needs them, or to purchase a special heart-lifter gift for the elderly lady on a limited pension. Then you can hear Jesus say to you, "I tell you the truth, whatever you did for one of the least of these brothers of mine, you did for me" (Matthew 25:40).

☑️ Escape the "Money Pit"

Many Christians today find themselves financially trapped. Money problems damage relationships, take away the joy of giving, provoke stress, and lead to overwork. If you want to use your money the way God intended, you'll want to heed the following advice:

1. Stay out of debt.

Never buy anything until you have the money to pay for it in full. Live by this rule and you'll save yourself a lot of problems. It's also good self-discipline, and curbs the impulse to spend.

Once you're saddled with a big debt, so many doors close. You can't go on the summer missions trips, or work less hours, or travel with your family to California, or give a special offering to help build a hospital in Africa. The money you owe makes you a slave. This is what's especially sad: You've sacrificed to buy things that will soon be worthless and have made it impossible for you to invest in people and projects that are of lasting or eternal value.

2. Don't evaluate others or yourself in terms of possessions.

"Man looks at the outward appearance, but the Lord looks on the heart" (1 Samuel 16:7). As children of our heavenly Father, we too must learn not to judge by the quantity of a person's possessions but by the individual's quality. Whenever clothes, cars, pastimes, or nice houses become the ruler by which we measure others, we're way offtrack.

To think according to God's standards, you must constantly renew your mind with Scripture. Every advertisement assures you that you need to buy something more to be cool, or to appeal to the opposite sex, to be acceptable in public. The devil is constantly sewing seeds of inferiority that are designed to make you feel out of place if you're wearing cheap jeans, you don't have the money to go on the band trip, or your dad works as a mechanic. Whenever you feel compelled to go into debt to buy something really sharp so that others will notice you—*stop*! Find a place to be alone with Jesus. Let Him affirm your self-worth.

Remember: If you had a million dollars to spend on clothes, cars, or recreation, it wouldn't make you a better person. Instead, do all you can to become a person after God's own heart— a goal that doesn't require big bucks.

3. Don't freeload.

"If a man will not work, he shall not eat" (2 Thessalonians 3:10). This is a very important biblical principle. Paying your own way and pulling your own weight is part of obeying God. There is no place in the life of a Christian for self-centeredness, taking advantage of others, or stinginess. Returning what you borrow promptly, paying back any money you owe, and treating the possessions of others with respect is part of your Christian testimony.

Responsibility and generosity are important to God and should be important to you.

4. Exercise self-discipline.

The little kid who gets everything he wants soon becomes unbearable. Yet our society teaches us to feel sorry for ourselves if we want to buy something and can't afford it.

If your parents spoiled you, then learning to wait or to deny yourself will be even harder. But the discipline of living within a strict budget will also build strong character and maturity. It will allow you more freedom to serve God, an ability to appreciate more what you do buy, and will prepare you for a more successful marriage.

Handling money God's way presents both a challenge and an opportunity. If you decide money matters strictly on biblical principles, your financial life can be a happy one.

☑ Setting Your Goal

1. Check the objectives you'd like to work on:

☐ I want to make it my goal to give to God ten percent of all the money I receive.

☐ I want to stop measuring my self-worth by the clothes I wear, the car or bike I own, and the things I possess.

☐ I want to stop buying things on credit.

☐ I want to put godliness-with-contentment-is-great-gain into practice.

☐ I want to be thankful for everything God provides—even if my friends have a lot more than·I do.

☐ I want to learn to apply self-discipline so I can live within my budget.

☐ I want to be careful not to take advantage of anyone and to pay my own way.

2. Write out specific financial goals and first steps for attaining them.

My financial goals are: _____

_____

_____

_____

_____

_____

The first step will be _____

_____

_____

Signed, _____

8
Say Yes to Life!

God's Gift of Life

You go to biology class and hear that human life began as the result of eons of evolution guided by random selection that produced from inorganic matter everything from protoplasm to people. In social studies you discuss pro-choice, which is interpreted to mean that any woman any time can rid herself of "unwanted tissue" by means of abortion. Although you did hear in health class that alcohol and drugs are bad for your body, the Friday after-school conversations center around parties—at which everyone intends to get bombed and buy supplies of drugs for the weekend.

When your dad turns on the TV/evening news, you discover that the "right to die" when and how you choose is being considered as an addition to Americans' "inalienable rights." A growing number of people believe that because there are insufficient funds for adequate health care for all, the retarded and severely physically handicapped should be ignored or eliminated, since they supposedly contribute nothing to society and don't enjoy a quality of life worth maintaining. . . .

The suicide machine . . . gang murders . . . free-basing cocaine . . . anorexia . . . there are so many messages that indicate most people don't think life is worth much.

You have a choice to make: You can choose to simply absorb the thinking of those around you, accepting the dirt-cheap price tag they put on human life, or you can seek out God's truth and live by it. This decision is a critical one that will affect your life now, in time, and in eternity.

When the Israelites received the Lord's review lesson on His commandments, these words were included: "I have set before you life and death . . . now choose life" (Deuteronomy 30:19). Rejecting God and His guidelines for living means spiritual suicide, and it can also mean physical impairment or death.

You've got to know what's going on here: Behind the philosophies that degrade human existence is Satan himself—and Jesus called him the thief who "comes only to steal, kill, and destroy." The devil loves it when people commit suicide, when kids ruin their minds and shorten their lives with drugs, when a girl becomes so obsessed with being thin that she starves herself to death, and when young people are told that they sprang into existence from the muck by a quirk of fate, so their lives don't really count for anything anyway.

It is *essential* that you learn the truth. Only truth will help you see the deceptions of Satan, the father of lies, exposed for what they are.

☛ Human Life Is Very Valuable for the Following Reasons:

1. God created the universe and each person who is part of it with purpose and design.

Every human being—even those who came into the world through illicit sex, even those who are severely handicapped, and even those born into incredibly difficult circumstances—can say with the psalmist, "For you [God] created my inmost being; you knit me together in my mother's womb" (Psalm 139:13). You are not a product of a chance combination of atoms of unexplainable origin, which over billions of years evolved into human form. A loving God allowed you to be born into the world in order to have a chance to accept Jesus as your Savior so you could enjoy eternal life with Him. There is a wonderful purpose and a great future planned for you: You can accept it or reject it. Your life, and the lives of the other four billion inhabitants of this planet, is an incredible opportunity.

2. Life on earth is meant to prepare you for eternal life.

If there were no life after death, human existence could be pretty meaningless. It would be extremely difficult to explain suffering, shattered dreams, and bad breaks. We were born into space and time, yet God wants to ready us to live in another dimension. So He allows earthly agony in order to accomplish heavenly purposes. God has ways of letting us know when our actions are keeping us from following the narrow road that leads to life eternal. Getting drunk is followed by a hangover. Illicit sex brings venereal diseases. God doesn't interrupt His natural laws to make sure that no child is born out of wedlock, but He does have a wonderful plan for that little person. Rebellion against earthly authority creates problems, just like disobeying any of God's other commandments. War, crack babies, divorce, government scandals, and vandalism are all the result of somebody's sin. Seeing these things should make us realize that human wisdom is faulty, and it should drive us to God for answers. He uses even evil and its devastating results to show His power, comfort, and truth. And He promises "in all things God works for the good of those who love him."

But if we reject God, we really seal our own doom. We are warned: "If you do not obey the Lord your God and do not carefully follow all his commands and the decrees I am giving you today, all these curses will come upon you and overtake you" (Deuteronomy 28:15). Consequences for sin are built into the universe.

Sometimes, I'm afraid, the only way God can get our attention is through tragedy. A friend recently told me this sad story. Although he grew up in a fine Christian home, he was a rebellious and proud fifteen-year-old. One day he went mountain climbing with his cousins and some friends. During the climb, a big boulder fell on his leg, crushing it and leaving him in excruciating pain. To carry him down the mountain on a homemade stretcher took hours. The pain grew so intense he was screaming. Even non-Christians in the group told him he should pray, but his hardened attitude of self-sufficiency prevailed.

When they reached a hospital, he was operated on immediately. Several hours after he regained consciousness the terrible truth struck him. They had amputated his leg! Now the pain was in his heart. The life he had planned for himself, full of sports and physical activity, was gone forever. He began to sob. It was only after all this that he needed God. Ladies from church who were visiting the ward urged him to accept Christ. He did and he has been a tremendous Christian ever since. Hard as it sounds, he'll tell anybody that losing a leg in order to find Christ was worth it.

God made us, and He understands our every thought and reaction, even though we don't. And He knows how to best design our circumstances to give us the opportunity to seek Him with our whole hearts. But so many people come to that crucial decision point and still choose hardness, bitterness, and rebellion instead of surrendering to God.

The trials, temptations, and tragedies of human existence in no way make life less worthwhile; they give us our best chances to contemplate the major purpose for life in the first place—offering us an opportunity to prepare for heaven.

3. God has designed each person with intrinsic value that does not depend on performance.

In God's sight the fetus of two months is just as important as the President of the U.S. The brilliant executive is not worth more than the little old lady confined to a wheelchair. (In fact, she may be advancing God's kingdom with her prayers, while he may be ruining lives with his ruthless business practices.) The retarded girl who tries to sing "Jesus Loves Me" brings more joy to Jesus than the famous rock star whose fantastic voice and technically great guitar playing serves Satan by promoting sick and promiscuous values.

The apostle John tells us of a song of praise to God that is sung in heaven. It goes like this: "You are worthy, our Lord and God, to receive glory and honor and power, for you created all things [no exceptions] and by your will they were created and have their being" (Revelation 4:11). How freeing and reassuring to realize that you—and everybody else—is infinitely valuable to God even if other people don't think you're smart, or good-looking, or productive, or cool.

4. The God who created you has a plan for your whole life, even if you yourself can't see that purpose.

I'd just gone with my mother to visit my grandmother in the rest home. I wasn't quite prepared for what I saw—shriveled-up old people walking with canes, one lady who constantly got lost, another confined to a wheelchair, a man yelling incoherently. I couldn't get the scene out of my mind and kept asking God, "Why?"

Then it came to me. Old age is like a neon light that no one can avoid seeing, and it really says: "Prepare to meet your God." It gives independent, strong-willed people a warning that life is ending and they have one last chance to get right with their Creator. The life of every elderly or terminally ill person has a very important purpose.

Your life, too, is *significant*. Yes, it's much better to avoid the pitfalls of sin in the first place. But there is nothing you can do that is so bad that God can't redeem your life and give it real meaning. And every life, from conception to death, is part of God's incredible plan. Ending life prematurely interrupts that divine design.

If you accept biblical Christianity, life is most valuable indeed. Each person who has received Jesus as Savior can say with David, "The Lord will fulfill his purpose for me" (Psalm 138:8). You were born with a life mission, something special to contribute to the kingdom of God. It can be as exciting as being President of the United States or Queen of England. Why? Because you and I have the privilege of being the temple of the Holy Spirit.

That treasure of power, love, joy, and peace within should remind you that everything you say and do makes a difference because the Creator of the universe has filled your heart with His Spirit.

As a Christian your existence has vast meaning and importance.

Another reason why life is worthwhile for the born-again believer in Jesus is because he or she can measure temporal setbacks and problems in the light of eternity. There will be heavenly prizes for earthly faithfulness. "And if anyone gives even a cup of cold water to one of these little ones because he is my disciple, I tell you the truth, he will certainly not lose his reward" (Matthew 10:42). Even when you stand out from the crowd and feel so alone, you can know that someday it will be worth it. "Blessed are you when people insult you, persecute you and falsely say all kinds of evil against you because of me. Rejoice and be glad, because great is your reward in heaven" (Matthew 5:11–12). Jesus tells us to love our enemies and promises, "Then your reward will be great" (Luke 6:35).

Even the most boring, everyday routine of classes, study,

and work has meaning because Jesus sees what you do. "Whatever you do, work at it with all your heart, as working for the Lord, not for men, since you know you will receive an inheritance from the Lord as a reward. It is the Lord Christ you are serving" (Colossians 3:23–24). Because of all this, Jesus said, "I have come that they may have life, and have it to the full" (John 10:10).

Jesus offers a never-ending supply of abundant life, and it's available to those who come to Him often enough and stay long enough to fill up their tanks.

You may be thinking, "I know all that. And when I'm at home and at church I believe it. But at school *no one* thinks like I do, and there is unbelievable pressure to go along with the crowd."

Whoever said Christianity was for cowards? Being different isn't easy.

Think it over, and see how many everybody-else-does-it activities flirt with death—either directly or on the long-term installment plan. I'll bet it will help you resist temptation. Besides, God has all the power you need to do what is right. Just ask Him to pump you up.

The reasons for not drinking alcohol or taking drugs are good ones. "Drinking while driving is the number one teenage killer.[1] Although no one really knows whether he or she will become an alcoholic, starting to drink is playing Russian roulette. "Today

---

[1]Jerry Johnston, *Why Suicide? What Parents and Teachers Must Know to Save Our Kids* (Nashville: Oliver Nelson, 1987), p. 52.

there are 3.3 million teenage alcoholics in the United States."[2] "A teenage alcoholic, like any alcoholic, commits slow suicide."[3]

"By the end of high school, two-thirds of American teenagers have used illicit drugs"[4]—but you don't have to be one of them! According to the Surgeon General's report, *Healthy People,* teenagers are the only age group in the U.S. whose death rate has gone up in the last twenty years. There are two main reasons for this: alcohol and drug-impaired driving, and drug-related suicide.[5] Many teenagers have serious health problems because of substance abuse.

Premarital sex is not only wrong—*it can be fatal.* There are better things to do with your body. Don't let momentary pleasure and passing "acceptance" by your peers rob you of life or quality living.

"The horrible truth is that suicide is America's second greatest teenage killer."[6]

The notes left behind give a variety of reasons: difficult family situations, a feeling of rejection, broken romances, drug addiction, and hopelessness, to mention a few. One boy put it this way in his suicide note: "I'm sorry, but the devil has my mind and I must escape him before I do something wrong."[7]

Behind every temptation is Satan himself—telling Eve to eat of the forbidden fruit, urging a young girl to jump into the backseat of the car with her boyfriend, or suggesting that suicide is the way out. The devil is always a liar. Suicide is *never* the only exit. God is God. He made the universe, and your most painful problem won't confuse Him.

Like any temptation, suicide begins as an idea placed in your mind. And it's dropped there in such a clever way that you often assume you're the one who's responsible for it. The devil next tries to convince you to buy his idea and make it your own. At this point you have to make a decision—either you reject the thought or you take it and run with it. More precisely, you take it and die with it. Although you may *feel* powerless to exercise

[2]*Why Suicide?*, p. 54.
[3]*Why Suicide?*, p. 55.
[4]*Why Suicide?*, p. 59.
[5]*Why Suicide?*, p. 65.
[6]*Why Suicide?*, p. 34.
[7]*Why Suicide?*, p. 113.

your will, you can turn your attention in another direction—*if* Jesus lives in you.

The Bible gives very important promises for times like these. You should memorize them and claim them often. "Submit yourselves, then, to God. Resist the devil, and he will flee from you" (James 4:7). "The one who is in you is greater than the one who is in the world" (1 John 4:4). Don't think you're immune from the temptation to end your life. It can come to anyone. The devil can cleverly concoct a seemingly hopeless situation and then tempt you to kill yourself. Prepare to reject the idea the moment it surfaces.

God called His creation good. He's proud of us—"Everyone who is called by my name, whom I created for my glory, whom I formed and made" (Isaiah 43:7). He loves you so much that He sent His only Son to die for you. He designed time and eternity so He could share His forever with you. Paul talks about "the riches of his glorious inheritance in the saints" (Ephesians 1:18). The grace and love that He has invested in us will bring Him glory and enjoyment forever. You were not made for suicide. You are part of the only inheritance God has!

A lot of teens forget that suicide is for keeps. It permanently blanks out all your potential, and it inflicts lasting emotional wounds on family and friends. Most suicide attempts are "unsuccessful," but many will leave you with life-long handicaps. And unintentional deaths often result, even though the victim had another goal in mind.

When things seem hopeless, don't even consider suicide. *God has a way out for you.* Have the courage to talk the problem over with a caring person—preferably a mature Christian. Call a friend, a pastor, or a crisis intervention center. Say *no* to Satan's suicide scheme for you.

And then there is Satan's scheme to involve you in premarital sex and all its pitfalls. Although it is much better to follow God's rule, which prohibits all sex except within marriage, decide *now* that abortion will never be an option for you. Having a baby or fathering a child outside of wedlock isn't at all easy. But there are people who will help, and it's possible to put that precious little one into a good adoptive home. There will be emotional wounds to deal with, but they'll be less severe than the guilt, the trauma, and the scars that result from an abortion. "You shall not kill" also includes your baby.

But Satan whispers, "Just get rid of that unwanted fetus. No one will know!"

God says, "He who conceals his sins does not prosper, but whoever confesses and renounces them finds *mercy*" (Proverbs 28:13). Nothing freezes and kills a soul like murdering another human being and going on as if nothing has happened. Honestly confessing sin and owning up to what you've done is the way to find pardon, peace with God, and a new lease on life.

You do not have the "right" to kill an innocent baby—regardless of what today's feminist leaders say. The Lord declares, "See now that I myself am He! There is no god besides me. I put to death and I bring to life" (Deuteronomy 32:39). He doesn't appreciate any competition! Trying to play God is very dangerous.

What if you do fall into fornication and a little person made in the image of God begins to form inside you? Have the courage to choose life, to decide on true repentance. If you do, you will also choose emotional freedom.

Somehow the greatest mortal sin of today is to be "uncool." So many swallow the cruel lie that if they can't be totally awesome, it'd be better to evaporate—so they stay high in order to avoid having to face the facts, or they try to make it with enough girls or guys to "prove" themselves, or they commit suicide. The belief of the hour is this: Only popular people count; you're out of it if you don't wear the right clothes, use current expressions, think politically correct, perform perfectly, and conform to the subculture—even though it means giving up your individuality, your freedom, and your Christian standards. The price of this misleading mentality (borrowed from and supported by the adult world) is monumental.

Today's thinking tells us that the elderly, the retarded, the terminally ill, the handicapped, and the misfits are to be tolerated, ignored, or ridiculed—but never accepted as people worthy of respect. Some even go so far as to suggest that these "unproductive" people would be better off dead and that society should make the decision for them.

This philosophy also makes it very difficult for the individual to cope with failure and disappointment. If you're conditioned to think of "noncontributing" citizens as a nuisance, it's pretty easy to transfer that opinion to yourself whenever you don't measure up. That nagging fear that you're not attractive enough, or bright enough, or rich enough, or talented enough can cause a lot of unnecessary agony.

✔ The Goal Is Freedom From the World

Lining up your attitudes with God's truth is so refreshing and so freeing. Your value is based on this fact: that a caring God created you special, and loved you so much that He sent His only Son to die for you. How good-looking, or smart, or productive you are doesn't matter to God. Some of the qualities that Jesus considered most important to happiness and well-being are patience, a longing after what is right, kindness, purity, peacefulness, and integrity in living—and they are qualities available to all. Even if your peers put you down for living these Christian values, they will contribute to your inner joy and contentment. Jesus didn't choose His disciples because they were popular, successful, and well-dressed. He wanted men who were willing to leave everything in order to follow Him. *His standards haven't changed.*

God loves you and accepts you as you are because He sees your great potential. And that potential is based only on how willing you are to let Him live His life of love and peace and power through you. Paul explained this principle to Corinthian Christians:

> Brothers, think of what you were when you were called. Not many of you were wise by human standards; not many were influential; not many were of noble birth. But God chose the weak things of the world to shame the strong. He chose the lowly things of this world and the despised things—and the things that are not—to nullify the things that are, so that no one may boast before him. It is because of him that you are in Christ Jesus, who has become for us wisdom from God—that is, our righteousness, holiness and redemption. Therefore, as it is written: "Let him who boasts boast in the Lord." (1 Corinthians 1:26–31)

Jesus is everything you need to have an enjoyable and fulfilling stay on this planet. You can decide to go it on your own, or to make it through with Him. "I have set before you life and death, blessings and curses. Now choose life."

✔ Setting Your Goal

Check the *incorrect attitudes* you've picked up somewhere along the line:
- ☐ I got here by chance.
- ☐ The main purpose of life is success and happiness.
- ☐ Only healthy, productive people count.
- ☐ A human fetus isn't a person and has no rights.
- ☐ I better live it up now because old age has nothing to offer.
- ☐ What I do doesn't really matter.
- ☐ Only the here and now is important.
- ☐ Taking drugs and drinking alcohol is part of being a teenager.
- ☐ I could never be tempted by suicide.
- ☐ If you're suicidal, there's no way to resist it.
- ☐ Sometimes suicide is the only solution.
- ☐ A mother has the right to kill her unborn baby.
- ☐ My worth depends on what I can achieve.

In your own words rewrite the false statements above to make them true. If you can, find a Bible verse that disproves each wrong idea and write the reference. (Or use those that follow.)

_____

_____

_____

_____

_____

_____

_____

_____

_____

_____

_____

_____

_____

_____

_____

_____

_____

_____

Signed, _____

1. Genesis 1:27
2. Ephesians 1:11, 12
3. 1 Corinthians 1:27–31
4. Psalm 139:13–16; Jeremiah 1:4–5
5. Proverbs 16:31; 17:6
6. Galatians 6:9; Revelation 20:12
7. Matthew 7:13–14; 12:36
8. 1 Corinthians 6:20
9. 1 Kings 19:3–5; Jonah 4:9
10. 1 Corinthians 10:13
11. Jeremiah 32:26–27
12. Deuteronomy 32:39
13. Romans 5:8; Luke 23:40–43

9
The Sexual *Revelation*

Did You Know That the Dating Game Has Rubs?

A delicious turkey dinner with all the trimmings served with your choice of three kinds of pie. . . . Sounds great! But what if someone invited you out to eat—at your local landfill? Some settings are better than others.

Sex, like that turkey dinner, cannot be properly appreciated unless it's experienced under right circumstances. The girl who wonders, "Will he still love me tomorrow?" can't really enjoy sex. Frantically forcing some experience, hoping not to get caught, robs you of its fullness. Fearing an unwanted pregnancy, young lovers can't freely give themselves to each other. Knowing you'll be compared to other sexual partners and having to prove yourself produces stress and frustration. God created sex for the security of a loving marriage relationship.

Experimentation, trial and error, broken hearts, damaged emotions, and incurable diseases are the legacy of our if-it-feels-good-do-it-now society. "If present trends continue, fully 40 percent of today's fourteen-year-olds will be pregnant at least once before age twenty."[1]

"Currently, 45 percent—almost half of teenage girls who become pregnant have an abortion."[2]

"Sexually transmitted diseases (STDs) are record high levels among teens."[3]

The list of alarming statistics goes on and on.

Is there a way out of this so-called "sexual revolution"?

There is. It's the sexual *revelation*. It's found in the Bible and it's been there for centuries. Jesus had this to say:

---

[1]Jerry Johnston, *Why Suicide? What parents and Teachers Must Know to Save Our Kids* (Nashville: Oliver Nelson, 1987), p. 44.
[2]*Why Suicide?*, p. 43.
[3]"The Dangers of Doing It," *Newsweek,* Special Edition (Summer/Fall 1990), p. 56.

"Haven't you read," he replied, "that at the beginning the Creator 'made them male and female,' and said, 'For this reason a man will leave his father and mother and be united to his wife, and the two will become one flesh'? So they are no longer two, but one. Therefore what God has joined together, let man not separate." (Matthew 19:4–6)

"It is God's will that you should be holy; that you should avoid sexual immorality; that each of you should learn to control his own body in a way that is holy and honorable, not in passionate lust like the heathen." (1 Thessalonians 4:3–5)

"You shall not commit adultery." (Exodus 20:14)

"Flee from sexual immorality. All other sins a man commits are outside his body, but he who sins sexually sins against his own body. Do you not know that your body is a temple of the Holy Spirit, who is in you, whom you have received from God? You are not your own; you were bought at a price. Therefore honor God with your body." (1 Corinthians 6:18–20)

Following the commandments of God's *sexual revelation* will give you a lot more real joy and fulfillment than falling for the lies of the sexual revolution. The God who made you knows what will bring you the most lasting happiness. God has some very good reasons for His rules.

☑ Why Wait Until Marriage to Have Sex?

1. *Your life and your health may depend on it.*

An article by Sonia L. Nazario in a recent issue of the *Wall Street Journal* states: "One in seven teens nationwide contracts a sexually transmitted disease, and a growing number are infected with HIV."

Dr. James Dobson discusses the health reasons behind chastity until marriage. He declares that there is no such thing as "safe sex" and backs it up by citing that the British Medical Journal reported that the overall failure rate of condoms due to slippage and breakage was *26 percent*. He also explained that the HIV virus is so very small that condoms are not considered capable of preventing its spread. He further documents his case. "I'm sure this explains why not one of 800 sexologists at a recent conference raised a hand when asked if they would trust a thin rubber sheath to protect them during intercourse with a known HIV-infected person." Dobson worries that because these facts are withheld from American teens, many will suffer the rest of their lives for practicing what they thought was "safe sex."

Dobson says he "deplores" the casual way with which sex is treated in the media. "Of course, the beautiful young fornicators in those steamy dramas never faced any consequences for their sin. No one ever came down with herpes, or syphilis, or chlamydia, or pelvic inflammatory disease, of infertility, or AIDS, or genital warts, or cervical cancer. No patients were ever told by a physician that there was no cure for their disease or that they would have to deal with the pain for the rest of their lives. No one ever heard that the human papilloma virus (HPV) kills more women than AIDS, or that a strain of gonorrhea is now resistant to antibiotics. No, there was no downside. It all looked like so much fun."[4]

What's really going on here? There are some folks who want to keep you in the dark.

Because people want to sell condoms, defend their promiscuous lifestyles, and fit in with "modern morality," they keep all these things secret. But the traps and dangers are there all the same. Sleeping around is very dangerous to your health. It could even kill you.

2. *Waiting preserves the beauty and richness of an experience created for two permanent partners.*

Today's teenage sexual activity has almost nothing to do with real love, commitment, and respect. "Planned Parenthood's own data show that the number one reason teenagers engage in intercourse is *peer pressure*. There is more pressure than ever for a girl to 'get it over with,' as one teenager put it."[5]

Allowing yourself to be conned into having sex just the way you hop on a roller-coaster—because it promises to be a brief emotional high is really dumb. You can get off the roller-coaster and only be short some spare change. But that one sexual experiment might leave you with a child, an incurable illness, and some hard-to-handle emotional baggage. The risks are simply not worth it.

---

[4]James Dobson, *Focus on the Family Newsletter* (February 13, 1992).
[5]"The Games Teenagers Play," *Newsweek* (September 1, 1980).

Jerry Johnston, a nationally known leader who talks to thousands of teenagers each year, says this: "I have listened countless times to the anguished testimonies of emotionally damaged junior and senior high girls, forever scarred by 'good sex' that turned out to be so desperately bad. I've also heard tearful stories from guys who have failed in their sexual exploits and can't handle the embarrassment. Soured romantic relationships are a major factor in suicide attempts."[6]

Cheap thrills now are like withdrawals from the bank account of your future happiness. They are impossible to replace. You're entitled to a wedding night unmarred by shameful memories, guilt, and the hang-ups you picked up from previous sexual encounters. The news that you're an expectant mother or father should not remind you of the life you once snuffed out by abortion, or leave you wondering where the child you bore out of wedlock is now. You should be able to enter into marriage without your mate suspecting that since you cheated on God's moral standard in the past, you might do so again. Your spouse shouldn't have to fear that you're rating him or her against former sexual partners. Saving yourself for the husband or wife God has planned for you is a very wise investment that will pay big dividends.

God does forgive, and He does heal emotions. But no one will tell you that recovery from fast-lane living is easy. It does bring extra problems.

God requires chastity until marriage because He loves you and wants you to get maximum satisfaction and pleasure out of sex. He also wants to protect you against many deep emotional hurts.

3. Integrity is priceless.

Solid, healthy relationships between humans can be built only on trust. Whether it's friend to friend, girlfriend to boyfriend, husband to wife, teacher to student, boss to employee, business person to client, or President to public—the relationship can never be the same once confidence is lost. Many things can open a credibility gap—lying, cheating, hypocrisy, immorality, and broken promises are a few. Once a person doubts the integrity of another, things can never be the same.

Harry S Truman once commented that a man who is unfaithful

---

[6]*Why Suicide?*, p. 43.

to his wife is untrustworthy in every other area of life. A sizable percentage of citizens wouldn't vote for a man who is guilty of cheating on his wife. There are good reasons for these attitudes. The character flaws which cause moral looseness, whether before marriage or after, affect all other avenues of life.

☑ Inability to Keep God's Moral Law

1. Shows lack of self-control.

Solomon proclaimed: "Like a city whose walls are broken down is a man who lacks self-control" (Proverbs 25:28). Back in Bible days a city without walls didn't amount to much. It could be attacked and destroyed at will. You can never count on the person without self-control either. He or she will misspend the money, spew out hurtful comments, leave the work undone, give in to sexual temptation, or develop emotional dependency.

God does have a new beginning for you if this is your problem. It involves confession of sin and humbly obeying God as He takes you along a step-by-step process.

"For this very reason, make every effort to add to your faith goodness; and to goodness, knowledge; and to knowledge, self-control; and to self-control, perseverance; and to perseverance, godliness; and to godliness, brotherly kindness; and to brotherly kindness, love" (2 Peter 1:5–6). Peter adds that if anyone does not have these qualities, he has forgotten that he has been cleansed from his past sin.

2. Breaking God's laws indicates inability to plan the present in order to get the most out of the future.

An immoral act is always preceded by a bunch of foolish decisions. Sometimes the person just doesn't care and recklessly pursues passion. In other cases, the thrill of momentary pleasure tempts one to the point where it is no longer possible to put on the breaks. Sacrificing the future on the altar of the present leads to sex outside of marriage, large financial debts, hangovers, school dropouts, and lost jobs.

Amnon is a good biblical example of this kind of character. At first he was so desperately in love with Tamar that his frustration showed on his face. With his cousin's help, he made plans to seduce her. But Tamar was a girl with high moral standards, and she begged him to wait until he received permission from the king to marry her. Amnon refused to listen and, instead, raped her. Then he decided that he hated her.

Absalom, Tamar's brother, was so angry that he determined to get even. Absalom knew that Amnon couldn't resist an invitation to a good party—even one thrown by his enemy—and that he would drink to excess. So Absalom used the pleasure-now-pay-later character of Amnon to plot his murder.

Do you display this weakness? If so, remember that "the fear of the Lord is the beginning of knowledge." Study biblical principles and apply them until that rashness which automatically chooses the most attractive, the easiest, or the most exciting option without considering the consequences disappears from your mentality.

3. Breaking God's law reflects either manipulation of people or a basic insecurity.

Some people treat others as sex objects—playthings to be enjoyed for a time and then discarded for someone more exciting. Conning others into having sex, doing your work for you, or taking advantage of them in another way is part of this type of weak personality. The other side of the coin is the person who will go along with just about anything for fear of being rejected, considered uncool, or standing out from the crowd. If you can be morally compromised because not going all the way means you lose your boyfriend or a girlfriend, then you can be manipulated into other wrong behavior. Most illicit sex involves a manipulator and a person willing to be manipulated.

The cure for both defects is the same: Submit to God's standards and allow Him to give you His sense of self-worth. Then you will not need to manipulate others or give in to them.

4. Breaking God's law involves lack of self-respect and lack of respect for the other person.

The dictionary uses these words to define respect: honor, esteem, consideration, courtesy. If any of the following questions can't be answered in the affirmative, you are not showing respect:

100

- Will *both of us* feel good tomorrow and every day from now on about what we've done?
- Would *both of us* be happy if our actions were reported as headline news?
- Would *both of us* be content with all possible consequences of our actions?

The best definition of respect is found in Romans 12:9–10: "Love must be sincere. Hate what is evil; cling to what is good. Be devoted to one another in brotherly love. Honor one another above yourselves." Sex outside of marriage includes none of these ingredients.

5. *Breaking God's law requires you to cheat on a future marriage partner.*

There are so many people who, once they find the person they want to spend the rest of their lives with, would do anything to erase their past. *Don't join their ranks.*

If you've already blown it, remember that there is such a thing as secondary virginity. Receiving God's forgiveness and His power can reclaim lost territory. But that's a lot harder than just holding the line.

You can walk in victory. You can put on the righteousness of Jesus and let Him lead you into a godly marriage.

A word of warning for those who think, "I can be sexually active for a while and then repent whenever I decide to." The price tag for this type of callous disobedience is very high indeed. *You may never get that opportunity to change your ways.*

☞ Loving Jesus Enough to Obey Him Is Wonderfully Rewarding

Jesus said, "If anyone loves me, he will obey my teaching. My Father will love him, and we will come to him and make our home with him" (John 14:23).

When you really love someone, you want to please that person. It's unthinkable to declare, "I love you with all my heart"— and then go out and do the very thing that would most hurt that person. Paul says it this way, "Do you know that your bodies are members of Christ himself? Shall I then take the members of Christ and unite them to a prostitute? Never!" (1 Corinthians

6:15). The truth is that if you're caught up in promiscuity, you don't *really* love Jesus!

If you're willing to obey Jesus—even if it involves sacrifice and suffering—the indwelling Spirit of God will feel so much at home in your heart that He'll live His life through you. It's as if your willingness to obey installs the wires that conduct His power.

Jesus does have all power, and it's available for you to live in purity. You can tap into that power by deciding you will not make up your own rules or adopt the standards of the world. You *can* live by Romans 6:12–13:

> Do not let sin reign in your mortal body so that you obey its evil desires. Do not offer the parts of your body to sin, as instruments of wickedness, but rather offer yourselves to God, as those who have been brought from death to life, and offer the parts of your body to him as instruments of righteousness.

You can experience the joy and victory of presenting your body as a living sacrifice to God. When you give Jesus your love, He gives you back more than you could ever have imagined.

Decide on chastity until marriage. Or choose secondary virginity, which is also a beautiful gift to Jesus. Once you make this choice, some insights will prove useful.

First, most sin is made up of component parts—one added to another like Lego blocks until the tower is so high it's sure to fall. You always have several chances to say no before emotions are aroused beyond control. You could have chosen not to have watched the sexy video the night before. You could have decided not to date the person of questionable character. You could have declined to dress provocatively. You didn't have to go to a secluded place. You could have said no to prolonged kisses and petting. But when you pass up all those chances to say no, you won't be able to stop once you're already falling over the cliff. Saying *no* at point one is relatively easy. It gets harder as the road progresses. The King James Version of the Bible translates 1 Thessalonians 5:22 this way: "Abstain from all *appearance* of evil." That's powerful advice.

☛ Practical Suggestions for Maintaining Chastity

1. Realize that you'll never be able to resist temptation in your own strength. You'll always need God's power.

> So if you think you are standing firm, be careful that you don't fall. No temptation has seized you except what is common to man.

And God is faithful; he will not let you be tempted beyond what you can bear. But when you are tempted, he will also provide a way out so that you can stand up under it. (1 Corinthians 10:12–13)

Memorize these verses and apply them to your life. Read your Bible daily and learn verses by heart to keep your mind clean. If you don't replace the garbage you're exposed to with God's Word, it's pretty easy to lose the mental battle—and that's your first line of defense. Pray constantly, asking God to help you live in purity. Rely on God's unlimited resources, not your nearly depleted reserves, to walk in victory.

2. Choose friends who have high moral standards.

Dirty jokes, invitations to view pornography, talk about sexual experimentation, and pressure to engage in immorality is not what you need from your "friends." Instead, look for and pray for companions who will encourage you to follow God. Even if that good Christian whom you'd like to have as your friend lives across town, make the effort to keep up the relationship. If there's no group you can join that's not a bad influence, keep to yourself until God answers your prayer for a Christian friend. This requires courage but it's better than letting your peers drag you down.

3. Date only Christians.

If Christ really lives within you and you're a new creature, your goals are fundamentally different from those of a non-Christian. Wholeheartedly obeying God's Word with pure motives is your number one priority. A double life of pretense is unthinkable. Time spent in Bible study, prayer, and Christian fellowship is more fulfilling than other pastimes. Winning the world for Jesus is worth sacrificing time, money, and personal desires. These are not the heart-goals of any non-Christians.

If you're in a relationship with someone who has different spiritual goals, you're in a very dangerous situation. In order to make your relationship work, one of you has to compromise. Either you have to compromise your purpose for existing, or the non-Christian has to become a hypocrite—pretending to be interested in spiritual things when he or she is not. It also sets you up for heartbreak. "Hope deferred makes the heart sick, but a longing fulfilled is a tree of life" (Proverbs 13:12). First of all, you'll desire that your boyfriend or girlfriend become a Christian—which basically means that you're in love with what that person *could be*—not what he or she *is*. Sometimes a person wishes so hard that he or she becomes falsely convinced that the boyfriend or girlfriend really is a Christian.

Psalm 1:1 says, "Blessed is the man who does not walk in the counsel of the wicked." When you date someone, you automatically receive a lot of advice. Because you're anxious to please this very significant other, their counsel will become important to you. But ungodly advice has been the downfall of many people.

Making a commitment never to date a non-Christian will save you headaches and heartaches. If you get discouraged and are ready to compromise, just remember the story of Isaac (Genesis 24). There wasn't one girl in the whole country who worshiped the true God. Isaac was forty and still single. Reading how the Lord arranged for Rebekah to be his wife is sure to build your faith and encourage you to stand by your convictions.

4. Double date or plan activities with relatives or friends.

Including other people in your dates will keep things casual and reduce sexual temptation. It also gives you the opportunity to see how your date reacts in a variety of circumstances. It's extremely important to discover how he or she relates with family members. Attitudes toward parents reveal a lot about character.

Including friends of yours who aren't dating is a great chance to show unselfishness and Christian love. When you double date, go out with Christian couples who maintain the high standards you're striving for.

5. Carefully monitor what you read and see.

When scenes start to get sexy, either turn off the TV or switch channels. Be very choosey about the videos you rent and the movies you see. If you make a mistake, walk out or stop watching. Decide not to even open books or magazines that are designed to sexually arouse the reader.

Curiosity at this point can be your worst enemy. A Christian youth worker who ministered to gang kids in a big city tells of seeing a cheap novel in a garbage can in an alley. The devil's subtle suggestion came in a flash: "You could better understand these kids if you knew what they were reading." He then proceeded to read two pages of filth, which he had a terrible time erasing from his mind.

If you do fail at this point, confess it as sin—don't rationalize it away. Many times you can't help the first unintentional glance, but looking the second time or doing some investigation is your error. Memorizing Scripture is a proven technique for cleaning up a dirty mind.

6. Do your private talking in an atmosphere where there is little chance for temptation.

Parking on a lonely road at midnight, exploring a dark cave together, walking along a deserted beach in the moonlight, or sitting on the sofa at your house when everybody in the family has left for the weekend—this is asking for trouble! The two of you can share your dreams and ideas in more sensible settings. There are restaurants and outdoor cafes where you can sit and talk for hours. Take your walk on the beach in the afternoon, or invite another couple to go with you.

Be careful about praying together. It's all too easy to pray with your arms around each other in a secluded place—only to find out that the devil is just waiting for you to say "Amen" so he can zap you with the worst temptation ever. Leave room for Jesus to sit between you—literally—when you pray. Give all your attention to Him, not to each other.

7. Limit your expressions of physical affection.

Song of Songs 2:7 advises: "Do not arouse or awaken love until it so desires." If you have chosen chastity until marriage, it means that you will refrain from the long kisses, intimate embracing, and petting that arouse sexual desires. The devil will always tell you that you and your date are different than ordinary mortals and you're strong enough to engage in these pleasures without any problems. It's another of his lies designed to trap you. Don't fall for it.

Concentrating on the physical means that you don't get to know the other person very well mentally, emotionally, and spiritually—and these are the areas where any lasting relationship must be based. Someone has suggested a thirty-day is-your-relationship-solid test, and a longer time would make this exam even more valuable. Simply decide on no physical contact—not even holding hands—for a certain period of time. If you grow closer together without any dependence on the physical aspect of dating, your friendship probably has a future. But if you both lose interest, forget it.

By accepting God's *sexual revelation* and taking practical steps to guard your chastity, you're preventing heartbreaks and protecting your future marriage. Obeying God on this issue will give you peace and freedom.

☑ Setting Your Goal

Check your objectives:

☐ I will remain chaste until marriage.

☐ I will maintain my secondary virginity.

☐ I will choose friends with high moral standards.

☐ I will memorize verses that emphasize God's moral revelation (1 Thessalonians 4:3–8; 1 Corinthians 6:15–20; Romans 6:11–14).

☐ I will not intentionally look at anything that causes sexual temptation.

☐ I will date only born-again Christians.

☐ I will not permit any date to lure me to some secluded place.

☐ I will stay so close to Jesus that I want to obey Him, even if it means going against the crowd, or against another Christian who is weak.

☐ I will guard against too-close-for-comfort physical contact that could easily lead to moral compromise.

In your own words, write out the specific ways in which you intend to implement your goals:

_____

_____

_____

_____

_____

_____

_____

Signed, _____

10
Join the Human Race

Heaven Can Wait—Until God's Time for You to Go There!

It hits you in many different ways: Your parents are fighting again, and you feel helpless. Geometry is difficult, and it doesn't sink in no matter what you do. No one considers your opinion important enough to listen to what you say. You don't happen to be "cool" enough to compete with the popular kids at school. You feel so vulnerable to everyone's sarcastic comments. There's danger on the streets, and you feel defenseless.

Along comes someone with a book or course of meditation that guaratees you power over your circumstances. And you wonder—could it be true?

It's easy to fall for some New Age teaching that promises to put you in command of your own destiny. Plans for escaping the limitations of humanity have been around since the dawn of time. Egyptian pharaohs proclaimed themselves to be gods. Alexander the Great's mother taught him that he was divine—and he believed it, until he sat down and cried because there were no more worlds to conquer. There have also been magic rituals that were supposed to bring good luck, success, and riches. Archaeologists have even found a clay tablet in which a man threatens his "god" with starvation if he doesn't get what he wants!

All these things are making a big comeback. Meditation classes claim to help you discover the "god" within. Supposedly scientific methods of harnessing natural forces guarantee to enhance your personal power. Satanism offers the ability to dominate—at the price of submitting to demonic forces. A lot of people are buying in to it all.

Trying to control circumstances by some magic formula is becoming increasingly popular. There are candles to burn, spells to cast, rituals to participate in, phrases to chant, thought patterns to adopt, horoscopes to read, and even sacrifices to be made. Whether you wish to lure your boyfriend back, lose weight, take revenge, or get rich, somebody out there is offering unwary people a way to do it. Sometimes this mentality—"you can have it all"—even seeps into Christianity, and leaders hold out methods for supposedly getting all your prayers answered, avoiding all sickness, and for living in luxury. Others actually go so far as to tell you that you possess godlike qualities.

There is a desire deep within each of us to be more than human. God put that longing inside us, and He created heaven to fulfill this wish. But so many people want to take shortcuts. Because these quick fixes are laden with occult practices and danger, you should choose to avoid them. So right now you're imperfect, unable to cope with everything that comes your way, and likely to make quite a few mistakes. Well, join the human race. Heaven can wait—until God's time for you to go there.

☑ There Are Several Reasons Why the Teaching That Man Can Become God or That He Has God-like Qualities Is Contrary to Scripture

1. Human beings were created by God. We are not now and never will be "part" of God.

W. A. Pratney gives this answer to the question, "What is the difference between God and man?" "He [God] is uncreated and we are created. . . . His 'stuff' is absolutely and wholly different from ours—or anything else."[1]

---

[1]W. A. Pratney, *The Nature and Character of God* (Minneapolis: Bethany House Publishers, 1988), p. 27.

He also explains that man cannot *become* God: "It is impossible for the created to become *un*created. We had a point of beginning in created time; we are finite. God did not begin in time and is infinite."[2]

The psalmist defines God: "Before the mountains were born or you brought forth the earth and the world, from everlasting to everlasting you are God" (Psalm 90:2). He created man. "With my great power and outstretched arm I made the earth, and its people and the animals that are on it" (Jeremiah 27:5). Isaiah 29:16 has a message for those who say that all men are part of God: "You turn things upside down, as if the potter were thought to be like the clay! Shall what is formed say to him who formed it, 'He did not make me'? Can the pot say to the potter, 'He knows nothing'?"

2. Humans are sinful. God is not.

Instead of talking about it as a disease or an imperfection, "the Bible teaches us to regard sin as a specific kind of evil, as a moral evil for which man is directly responsible and which brings him under a sentence of condemnation."[3]

Scripture informs us that "all have sinned and fall short of the glory of God" (Romans 3:23). And, "If we claim to be without sin, we deceive ourselves and the truth is not in us" (1 John 1:8). God, on the other hand, is perfect: "Exalt the Lord our God and worship at his footstool; he is holy" (Psalm 99:5). The only righteousness we can receive is a *gift* from God. "God made him who had no sin to be sin for us, so that in him we might become the righteousness of God" (2 Corinthians 5:21).

3. Humans need the salvation that God gives.

Isaiah 45:22 states: "Turn to me and be saved, all you ends of the earth; for I am God, and there is no other." God provides our only salvation and it is completely His doing, not ours: "For it is by grace you have been saved, through faith—and this not from yourselves, it is the gift of God—not by works, so that no one can boast" (Ephesians 2:8–9).

---

[2]*The Nature and Character of God,* p. 27.
[3]Louis Berkhof, *Manual of Christian Doctrine* (Grand Rapids: Wm. B. Eerdman's Publishing Company, 1965), p. 138.

4. Humans, by nature, are fallible. God is not.

"God is not a man, that he should lie, nor a son of man, that he should change his mind. Does he speak and then not act? Does he promise and not fulfill?" (Numbers 23:19). People are complicated and undependable creatures. Even the apostle Paul gives this description of himself: "I do not understand what I do. For what I want to do I do not do, but what I hate I do" (Romans 7:15). How different is a definition of God. "He is the Rock, his works are perfect, and all his ways are just. A faithful God who does no wrong, upright and just is he" (Deuteronomy 32:4).

You will find that unscriptural teaching tries to: elevate man to the status of God; proclaim that you can attain your own salvation by doing something yourself; consider human reason the ultimate; ignore man's sinfulness and need for salvation. All of these ideas are designed to make people feel powerful. They make man, not God, the center of the universe, and obliterate the difference between God and His created beings.

At this time, New Age philosophy is growing in popularity. Because there is often an attempt to mix it with Christianity, the following distinctions will help you avoid its clutches:

1. Understand that Christ living in you is vastly different from the idea that you are God.

Once you invite Christ to take over your life, "this mystery, which is Christ in you, the hope of glory" (Colossians 1:27), begins. As a person "in Christ," you become a new creation. Mind-boggling! You are in Christ and Christ is in you—but you are *not* Christ.

The nature of God is holy and the nature of man is sinful. By believing and living in God's promise, we can "participate" in the divine nature—we can receive His righteousness, but we cannot become divine. True goodness never emanates from you. It's always borrowed from God. "His divine power *has given us* everything we need for life and godliness through our knowledge of him who called us by his own glory and goodness. Through these he has given us his very great and precious promises, so that through them you may participate in the divine nature and escape the corruption in the world caused by evil desires" (2 Peter 1:3–4).

We can become living water irrigation channels but never rivers. The truth we learn from God's Word forms the banks of the canal. The indwelling Holy Spirit who produces in us the life of Jesus is the *source* of the supernatural vitality which streams out from us to touch others. Although the life of Jesus is transmitted *through* us, we still know that Romans 7:18 is true— "nothing good lives in me, that is, in my sinful nature."

2. Realize the difference between God working through human beings in a supernatural way and a person supposedly "possessing" magical powers.

God worked so that when Elijah prayed, fire fell from heaven. After Peter and John told the crippled man to stand up, God did the miracle. At a Bible camp bonfire, as an older pastor gave a very simple message, a rebellious seventeen-year-old guy broke down sobbing. "I'm a sinner. I'm a sinner." I was aware that I was witnessing the supernatural. God was using a message with little teen appeal to bring conviction of sin.

No human can be God. "I can do all things through Christ which strengtheneth me" (Philippians 4:13, KJV). But that doesn't include things that are contrary to His will. And I can't do it by myself. Neither can you. *Depending completely on God,* you can accomplish incredible things. But all the love, all the power, all the ability, and the very air you breathe, come from the Lord of the universe.

3. Recognize that manipulating God and receiving answers to prayer are not the same thing.

God designed a system by which He works through humans to spread the gospel, to show compassion to the needy, and to accomplish His will on earth. It begins with us humbly praying for the things He wants to do. And He seldom breaks in to give a vision to the person who hasn't heard of Jesus, to rain down manna from heaven, or to send revival when no one has bothered to pray. Prayer moves God to act when He would not have otherwise done so, because this system is consistent with His sovereignty. Petitions that run contrary to His will don't count. The prayer God answers starts with God because it's based on His Word, His will, and the prompting of the Holy Spirit within.

Trying to manipulate God by using magic formulas (or "Christian" formulas) starts with man. It's a personal determination to control God or fate or the universal consciousness, or in some cases to placate the devil. It doesn't matter what you use—good luck charms, chain letters, rituals, or visualizing your prayers. If the *motive* is to be in control yourself instead of submitting to God, it's wrong.

Your decision in view of these facts should include both a positive and a negative aspect.

First, seek the legitimate power of the Holy Spirit—not to become important, famous, respected, and known for great accomplishments, but to live the Christian life displaying the fruits of the Spirit and to serve God in a dynamic way. "You will seek me and find me when you seek me with all your heart" (Jeremiah 29:13). This is the biblical method of acquiring a strong Defender when things get tough. The quest must continue: "Ask and it will be given to you; seek and you will find; knock and the door will be opened to you. . . . If you then, though you are evil, know how to give good gifts to your children, how much more will your Father in heaven give the Holy Spirit to those who ask him!" (Luke 11:9, 13).

This is not a quick fix. It's a lifetime of learning to receive more and more Holy Spirit power to overcome Satan, to witness to others, to love unconditionally, and to obey God by taking scary steps of faith. This doesn't usually bring great wealth or fame, but it gives you a life filled with excitement, purpose, and contentment.

Second, you should reject all desires for obtaining power and recognition for personal goals. Don't dream about being the leader everybody wants to follow, the hero or heroine who captures the headlines, or the controller of every situation. Avoid all superficial and unscriptural ideas that promise to put you in the driver's seat. Whenever you hear that there's a formula which enables you to call the shots, be suspicious. Ask for biblical passages to back up any teaching billed as new or deeper than "average" Christian doctrine. Use a concordance or topical

Bible to study all that God's Word says on the subject. Solicit the help of a mature Christian who knows the Scriptures better than you do. Even if everybody says the results are fantastic, *if it's not based on the Bible, forget it.*

Instead of trying to be a god, or a super-being, or a possessor of an organizationally controlled "secret to success," join the human race. In a word, accept your limitations—and God's great power at work within you. For only then can you be part of a great divine purpose: "But we [Christians] have this treasure [Christ] in jars of clay [our human bodies] to show that the all-surpassing power is from God and not from us" (2 Corinthians 4:7).

☑ Setting Your Goal

The following list of attitudes can be used by the devil in order to interest you in "power shortcuts." Check the ones that are problems for you:

☐ I'm desperate for attention, and need a way to show that I'm somebody important.

☐ I'm so discouraged and bored that I'll try almost anything for excitement.

☐ I'm tired of being told I don't meet God's standard. I'd like to hear that I'm okay without repenting.

☐ I'm sick of being inferior. I'll do anything to make my way to the top of the pile.

☐ God is too slow. I'd like to see some action.

☐ I don't like the way our youth group is run. If I were in charge, everything would be better.

☐ The pastor is too old-fashioned, but I know what our church needs.

☐ When I graduate, watch out. *I'm* going to turn the world upside down for Jesus.

☐ If it works, use it. Whatever is new and effective must replace the old. You can get too hung up on scriptural principles.

What I plan to do about dangerous attitudes I've discovered.

_____

_____

_____

_____

_____

_____

Signed, _____

What I plan to do if I'm presented with an ego-building, short-cut-to-power philosophy.

_____

_____

_____

Signed, _____

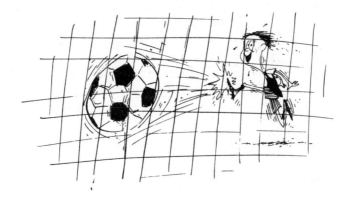

11
The Wonders of Witnessing

Don't Be a Secret Service Christian

When Tony came home from Bible camp he had big goals: He dreamed of giving his testimony in front of an all-school assembly; of leading the captain of the football team to Christ; of carrying his Bible to school; of organizing student prayer meetings. On the first day of classes, however, he was running so late that he forgot to take even a pen and a notebook. Bringing his Bible never crossed his mind. It was third hour before he remembered his plan for the new school year.

Then the new biology teacher began: "I'm not one of those guys who thinks that the first man was made out of dust, that the first woman was once a rib, that the snake talked, and that the first jeans were made out of fig leaves—okay?"

Everybody laughed.

"If you do believe all this stuff," the teacher continued, "please raise your hand, because you and I are going to have some differences."

Tony felt as if his hand was paralyzed. All eyes scanned the room to see who the "geeks" were. Tony could not do anything but stare at the floor.

Lunchroom conversation made fun of those kids who didn't fit the drugs, sex, and rock-and-roll mold. It presented Tony with a perfect chance to explain real Christianity—but he remained silent. He convinced himself that nobody at his school was ready to listen to the gospel.

After that, the Jesus-Is-the-Answer T-shirt stayed in the drawer. He turned into a secret service Christian. If there were other believers at his school, they must have assumed the same role—avoiding the really bad stuff, but hoping that no one would ever find out how really different they were.

It's easy to be a Peter, vowing even to die for Jesus only to deny Him completely because it's the socially acceptable thing to do.

Teenagers sure don't have a monopoly on this type of behavior. A pastor I knew commented that so many people identify with Peter before the day of Pentecost, but very few claim to be like him after he became convinced of the authority of the risen Christ. Then Peter was personally empowered by the Holy Spirit to spread the gospel, and he and his fellow apostles were accused of turning the world upside down. His life—and that of D. L. Moody, Charles Wesley, Amy Carmichael, and so many others—was totally transformed by letting go of a carefully protected self-concept and fully surrendering to what the Holy Spirit wanted to accomplish in them. But trying to witness in your own strength will burn you out.

Seek to know God in deeper and deeper ways and to fully depend on Him. Only then can the power of the Holy Spirit within you be let out of the cage that your inflexible personality or your fear of people have built around Him.

A willingness to let God use you to win others to himself involves yielding to God your right to be popular, to always have others think well of you, to live selfishly, to avoid suffering, and to be lazy about your Bible study. If you really want to become an effective witness for Christ, you'll have to cooperate with Him in several areas:

☛ Be Willing to Be Delivered From the Fear of What Others Will Think of You

Although this doesn't mean you dress funny, speak in born-again jargon, and act like an oddball, it does involve receiving from Jesus the courage to stand alone—and even to appear ridiculous at times. As long as you stay in the chameleon-Christian-conforming-to-the-culture mold, God won't be able to use you very much. And allowing the Lord to break your people-pleasing posture will involve pain and embarrassment.

This doesn't usually happen overnight.

I was a history teacher in public high school, and God gently and graciously led me to take steps of faith until it didn't matter to me what anybody thought. I wondered what the kids would say about my putting a Bible on my desk, but I obeyed God. It wasn't very easy to propose that I teach a Bible history class to the outspoken atheist who was chairman of the department. But through circumstances, he got fired, and fifty-five students signed up for my course.

I felt embarrassed when a decidedly uncool sophomore came in every morning to read the Bible out loud to me as my seniors were arriving for homeroom. But I didn't have the heart to discourage him, and God was chipping away at my desire to appear at least a little bit "awesome." Putting invitations in the boxes of the women faculty members for an evangelistic lunch-eon, I could only imagine what would be said behind my back. But some teachers came, and one accepted Christ.

The neat thing about letting God break down all our defen-siveness is that it puts within others a genuine respect for you. The day came when the most unruly of my sixth-hour sopho-mores used the last three minutes of class to get down on their knees and simulate an exaggerated version of a "holy-roller" prayer meeting and announce that this was what I did every Saturday night! When they said, "Praise the Lord," I could hon-estly in my heart praise the Lord anyway! Another day, a drug-gie brought his friend all the way up to my third-floor room to stare at me as though I were an exhibit in the city museum. "I ain't never seen a Puritan before," he said mockingly, and then left. I could actually smile, glad that God could use uncomfortable situations, embarrassment, and just plain craziness to free me from constantly having to guard my reputation.

Let God lead you along this path. Recently, I heard a radio report about a group of teenagers in a certain city who are carrying their Bibles to school and wearing T-shirts with evan-gelical messages. Because they didn't buckle under the initial critical comments, the other kids were accepting them and ask-ing a lot of questions. This is one way of cooperating with God to come out of your Christian closet.

No matter how shy you are, God can deliver you from what I once heard Billy Graham call "the sin of fearing what other people will think." But you must be willing to pay the price. Don't ignore the problem. After all, if God's opinion is not more important to you than that of other people, something is radically wrong.

☑️ Realize That Once You Identify With Christ, Some People Who Are Running Away From God Will Avoid You

Being rejected isn't any fun. We all want our peers to like and respect us. When that doesn't happen, we tend to blame ourselves, concluding that we're unattractive, boring, socially unacceptable, or have bad breath. When we share Christ with a person who can care less, we easily pick up the idea that it's because we did something wrong.

Obviously we need to present the gospel well and maintain a good testimony. But we must also face the reality of spiritual warfare. Some people are fighting God. If you remind these individuals of God, they will take out their hostility on you. Jesus himself experienced this and reminds us that the same thing will happen to us: "If the world hates you, keep in mind that it hated me first. . . . If they persecuted me, they will persecute you also" (John 15:18, 20). "When we verbally identify with the Lord Jesus Christ, those who reject Him and His standards will usually also separate themselves from us. The situation means that we do not reject them; they reject us."[1]

Never let the devil use this fact to ruin your self-image.

☑ Recognize That You Must Verbally Identify With Christ and Live a Life Pleasing to Jesus

A guy asked his pastor which was more important to his Christian testimony—his words or his life. The pastor responded, "Which wing on an airplane is more important, the right or the left?" Peter also put equal emphasis on the verbal expression of our faith and living it out in the day-to-day routine: "But in your hearts set apart Christ as Lord. Always be prepared to give an answer to everyone who asks you to give the reason for the hope that you have. But do this with gentleness and respect, keeping a clear conscience, so those who speak maliciously against your good behavior in Christ may be ashamed of their slander" (1 Peter 3:15–16).

There is no way people can automatically conclude that Jesus is the One who makes a difference in your life—unless you tell them. No one knows the way of salvation unless it is explained. "How, then, can they call on the one they have not believed in? And how can they believe in the one of whom they have not heard? And how can they hear without someone preaching to

---

[1]*Research in the Principles of Life Advanced Seminar Textbook* (Oak Brook, Illinois: Institute in Basic Youth Conflicts, 1986), p. 304.

them?" (Romans 10:14). God needs you to be His ambassador. People are missing heaven because no one has ever told them the truth from God's Word.

Learn to explain the gospel well, but remember that if your life doesn't back up what you say, your friends will be completely turned off.

☑ Get Evangelism Training

Since winning the world for Jesus is the most important project on earth, it makes no sense to study for a profession, go to swimming classes, take tennis lessons, learn French, finish driver's-ed, and not receive any instruction in evangelism.

You can start by memorizing a little booklet called "The Four Spiritual Laws,"[2] especially concentrating on the Bible verses.

When your church offers evangelism courses, take advantage of the opportunity. Go to a Christian bookstore and select some books to read on the topic. Though it's true that God can use even a poorly informed person to win another to Christ, your knowing what to say will give you confidence and make you much more effective.

You can also study the Bible to find the answers to the most

---

[2]Available from Campus Crusade for Christ, P.O. Box 628222, Orlando, Florida.

frequently asked questions. It's a good idea to keep a notebook with objections that come up and the Bible verses that apply. More than one person will tell you, "It doesn't matter what you believe as long as you believe it." Or "Jesus never claimed to be God."[3] You need to be able to point them to the Scriptures to resolve their confusion.

If you don't know the answer, find someone who does. You can tell the person you're sharing with, "That's a good question. I don't know the answer right now, but I'll find out and get back to you."

"Do your best to present yourself to God as one approved, a workman who does not need to be ashamed and who correctly handles the word of truth" (2 Timothy 2:15).

☑ Spend So Much Time With Jesus That You Hear His Voice

You can't really tell others that Jesus is your best friend if your days are so busy that you don't have at least a few minutes each morning and evening to be alone with Him. Unless you've received something new and fresh from God, you'll feel dry and have very little to share. The person who spontaneously declares what the Lord has done in their everyday life sparks interest in the gospel. People who like to know more about a God who improves your quality of life.

Daily Bible study and prayer are *essential* if you're to be an effective witness for Jesus. Pray every day for the unsaved people around you. Someone has well said, "You need to spend more time talking to God about people than talking to people about God."

You also need to communicate with God so you can discern His will. Impetuous evangelism projects, driven by human ingenuity, never pan out. Witnessing isn't a matter of dumping a sales pitch on any person you can corner: It's listening to God, so you can say the right thing to each person—not too much and not too little.

There are times when we are to remain silent, times when

---

[3] Verses to answer these objections: Acts 4:10–12; John 14:6; John 5:18; Matthew 26:63–64.

giving a tract would be inappropriate, and times when we must stop witnessing and just talk about other things. On other occasions, the person is ready for a complete gospel presentation, including a persuasive plea to accept Christ. But if you don't listen to God, you may try to harvest fruit that isn't ripe yet, or you may remain silent when you should have spoken.

Stay so close to God that you'll know what He wants for each situation.

✔ Don't Argue or Use Terms That Provoke Anger

Some of us are natural lawyers. We enjoy matching our wits with another to prove the person wrong. If you have this tendency, you must give up the delight you find in proving yourself right. Instead of smashing down the other person's argument with your superior logic, you can quietly say, "You know God's Word judges all of us. Let's turn to John 5:18 and see what the Scripture says about the topic." If you don't have a New Testament on you, give your reasons, and suggest that sometime the two of you get together to study the Bible.

Never make fun of what the other person says—no matter how weird. Always be courteous. Don't call the founder of his or her religion "despicable," or ridicule the fact that everybody in the sect has to wear a uniform. Let Ephesians 4:15 be your motto: "speaking the truth in love."

✔ Meet People Where They Are

If we're not careful, we can beat people over the head with the Bible, come on as know-it-alls, or condemn a person who doesn't know any better.

With compassion, we should try to put ourselves in the place of the other person. To some people, blatant sin is so normal that they don't even realize they're doing anything wrong. There are times we must begin by a demonstration of love, unaccompanied by any words, because the person has been totally turned off by Christianity. Others are so damaged by drugs and alcohol that it takes a long time for anything to sink in.

Being an ambassador for Christ requires great patience, unconditional love, unselfish concern, and wisdom that only God can give.

So many people have no biblical background. They need thoughtful explanations in language they can understand. Some are so wounded that they are reluctant to trust anyone—even Jesus. Building their confidence will take a lot of your time and your constant caring.

☛ Figure Out a Follow-up System

When people accept Christ, they're still babies and they need a lot of help. The love-'em-and-leave-'em approach needs improvement. Maybe the new Christian lives close to you, and you can help him or her study the Bible. Maybe you can invite the person to attend your church. If so, great. If not, it's important to get the individual's address in order to send follow-up material and personal letters of encouragement.

☛ Make an Eternal Difference

Reading through the requirements to be an effective Christian witness, you may be thinking, "But I don't want to be different. I don't like being in a goldfish bowl, where everyone notices every mistake I make. Self-sacrifice, rejection, hard study, and extra work—this isn't exactly what I'm looking for. I'd rather that no one outside my church know that I'm a Christian. Then I can have an enjoyable, relaxing ride to heaven."

But the tragic truth is that most people are traveling toward hell—eternal separation from God. And you can allow God to use you to rescue them. You've got the message that can save them. You're in possession of the secret that can free drug addicts, give hope to people who see no reason to live, and provide love for those who don't really know what the word means.

Standing up for Jesus is part of being a Christian: "Whoever acknowledges me before men, I will also acknowledge him before my Father in heaven. But whoever disowns me before men, I will disown him before my Father in heaven" (Matthew 10:32).

You're in the same position as the nurse, who holds a needle that can inject the vaccine that will stop the new virus threatening the lives of jungle tribesmen. Because they don't understand how a painful shot can help them, many usually refuse the offer. Often, the nurse can wonder why she's not at home swimming in her parents' pool, watching TV, and eating pizza.

But every afternoon this same woman finds new courage. Talking by two-way radio to the man she is planning to marry, she remembers that this charming young doctor convinced her to be one of the first people immunized by the vaccine he had discovered. When the first two cases of the deadly disease were admitted to the intensive care unit where she worked, the other two nurses were infected and died. She couldn't help but love the man who had saved her life and a beautiful romance developed between them. His passion to save the lives of as many people as possible became hers. His words gave her hope and determination to press on. They motivated her thoughts and inspired her actions. Slowly, one individual and then another understood and became willing to receive the injection. This brought her great joy, and more and more this work of saving lives became her reason for existing. The jungle was filled with other tribes that needed the medicine. Although she knew people would reject her, she wanted to make sure each person had the opportunity to be vaccinated against the killer plague. She had given up a lot, but she was happier than she had ever been before. She was an important person on a very strategic mission.

Become like that nurse. Fall in love with Jesus. Permit His priority—world evangelism—to become yours. Constantly draw strength from His Word. You'll find, like so many others, that even though the work is demanding and material rewards are few, this challenge makes life an adventure filled with delight and satisfaction.

✔ Setting Your Goal

Check the things you really want to do:
- ☐ Get more evangelism training.
- ☐ Study the Bible more.
- ☐ Memorize the verses that explain salvation.
- ☐ Pray more for non-Christians.
- ☐ Love people I find unattractive.
- ☐ Verbally explain the gospel to my friends.
- ☐ Become less self-conscious about standing out for Jesus.
- ☐ Be willing to be rejected because of my Christian testimony.
- ☐ Be willing to place myself in uncomfortable situations to share Christ.
- ☐ Be willing to invest time and care required to follow up the people I share with.

Concrete steps I plan to take that will enable me to more effectively share my faith with others:

_____

_____

_____

_____

_____

_____

_____

_____

_____

Signed, _____

12
You Mean I Have to *Study?*

The Rise and Fall of "Super Christian"

"Super Christian" did all the expected things: He attended every meeting at church, witnessed with an evangelism team, helped with the grade-school sports teams, and sang in the choir. But Spanish verbs, chemical equations, history dates, and English poetry bored him to death. He was always happy to find some excuse for not studying. Procrastinating until the last minute, "Super Christian" sometimes got his book reports off the cover, charmed a pretty girl for the answers to the history questions, copied from his friend's lab report, and even brought cheat-sheets to the Spanish tests. His grades were bad, but he thought his politeness, helpfulness, and excuses covered all his tracks.

Then something happened that shook him up. The youth group drama he starred in was presented at the outdoor theater in the park—and afterwards, he ran into his Spanish teacher.

"The play had some ideas worth considering," she commented, "but it's hard to respect the beliefs of someone who rarely does his homework—and who obviously cheated on the last exam. I know you did, because when I asked you some of the test questions in class, you didn't know any of the answers. Right now, if you asked me to become a Christian, the answer would be *no*."

This scenario has been repeated far too often. Only faithfulness, diligence, and integrity make your testimony believable. Besides, your life is not divided up into neat little compartments only one of which is "spiritual." When you invite Jesus to be the Lord of your life, He wants to rule in every area—including your studies and your work.

Most of your waking hours are spent on the campus or on the job.

Since our goal as Christians is to glorify God in all we do or say or think, a lot of what we believe must be lived out in these places. Dedicating your learning and work to God not only pleases Him—it's a fantastic testimony!

☛ Choosing to Discipline Yourself Is One of the Wisest Decisions You Can Ever Make

The following principles will help you to glorify God at school and at work.

1. Be more concerned about pleasing Jesus than getting the approval of your teacher or your boss.

If you study diligently for the algebra test to demonstrate love for Jesus, the D won't be such a disappointment. Praising God while cleaning the kitchen or the garage will make you more able to cope when your mom points out all the places you missed. Depending on Jesus to help you get through the first day as cashier will enable you to handle the pressure. If your boss doesn't notice the fact that you did more than your share of work, Jesus will. After your dad explodes because of your clumsiness, Jesus understands your intentions and thinks you did just fine. Although you did your best on the oral report, your teacher may be overly critical and crabby. But Jesus will give you an A. If the person in charge picks on you, Jesus will protect you if you do what's right.

Working for Jesus' approval instead of that of others can save you a lot of hurt feelings because Jesus is always fair. It helps us finish hard tasks because Jesus notices all the effort we put in even though no one else does. When we fail, the Lord—unlike those around us—knows what we meant to accomplish.

2. Remember that your studies and your job are training you to serve God.

There is nothing you can do in Christian work that doesn't require faithfulness and diligence. Helping on the cleaning committee, dishing up potato salad at the church picnic, ushering, serving on the youth council, teaching Sunday school, leading praise and worship—all require responsible and committed people. "Now it is required that those who have been given a trust [no matter how insignificant] must prove faithful" (1 Corinthians 4:2). "Whoever can be trusted with very little can also be trusted with much" (Luke 16:10). These are spiritual principles.

The devil has deceived many a Christian young person into

thinking like this: "School's not so important. Someday in the 'real world' I'll accomplish great things. Homework doesn't matter. I'd rather do the Lord's work." It sounds good on the surface, but it's only a way of covering your laziness, your boredom with routine, and your lack of initiative. It seems like a rather acceptable excuse, when in fact you work hard only on the things you *like* to do and *hate* being bossed around.

Jesus tells the parable of three servants who were given different quantities of money to invest for profit. The two who worked hard to double the original amount were commended, but the lazy servant was fired. He was neither obedient nor diligent. God is looking for people who, like the first two servants, seek Him in order to find out what He wants done. And then put their hearts into accomplishing it.

Effective Christian service "is not feverish activity of people whose restless dispositions keep them ever on the go . . . but the alertness of a diligent servant who has cultivated the upward gaze and can always see the Father's work that is waiting for his [or her] cooperation. . . . Christ needs workers who jealously guard the passing moments and never put off till tomorrow what can be done today. . . . Diligence is essential if we are to serve the Lord."[1]

Actually getting around to that algebra assignment, memorizing the parts of a plant, following your boss's instructions, and shoveling the sidewalk when your mother asks you to have a lot to do with your becoming someone God can count on to do His work. Everything that you accomplish—or leave undone— matters more than you'd ever imagine. Decide to add *diligence* to your character.

3. Realize that one of the most important investments in your future marriage, career, and happiness is learning how to be a good worker.

Most husbands don't enjoy coming home to a messy house, a dinner of potato chips and peanut butter sandwiches, and to a wife who doesn't like to leave her easy chair in front of the TV.

---

[1]Watchman Nee, *The Normal Christian Worker* (Hong Kong Church Book Room, LTD, 1971), p. 16.

And women get rather exasperated with spouses who constantly complain of working too hard on the job and who just never get around to making minor household repairs. When neither parent wishes to put the kids to bed, or carry out the garbage, or answer the telephone, life can be pretty rugged.

A lazy person automatically hates his or her job. Spending eight miserable hours each day is enough to wear anybody out. An ambitious person who looks for extra tasks that need doing enjoys going to work. Boredom and purposelessness characterize so many lives, but they have no place in the life of a hard worker. Because a diligent person keeps up with things, he or she rarely experiences the frustration of being so far behind that catching up seems literally impossible.

Learning to cheerfully clean up the kitchen, wash the car, do the unfair assignment, write the difficult term paper, or mop the floor at Taco Bell will give you the ability to demonstrate love to your future mate, to earn a promotion on the job, and to improve your quality of life.

4. Recognize that good study habits and hard work build character.

Have you ever baby-sat for a spoiled brat? It isn't that the kid's not cute and smart and really delightful—that is, when no unpleasant demands are made. The character flaw is that the child is unaccustomed to doing anything he or she doesn't feel like doing. The result is difficulties for the parents, problems for the child, civil wars between this kid and siblings, and a migraine headache for anyone who invites the whole family for dinner. Many adults have the same personality disorder. Taller, stronger, and more subtle, they're able to cause chaos wherever they go.

It's wise to decide to do everything possible to prevent your becoming Mr. or Ms. I'll-do-whatever-I-wish-to-thank-you.

Attacking and completing unpleasant tasks is part of character building. God knows this, so He allows parents, teachers, and bosses to dish out difficult homework, contemptible chores, and thankless tasks. All of these things give you a chance to learn faithfulness, perseverance, and integrity.

The problem is that no one thinks *positively* about these opportunities. When your mother says, "Clean out the closet," it never occurs to you that this is a marvelous occasion to learn diligence. If your teacher gives a long reading assignment for the weekend, when you planned to invite your friend to go cross-country skiing, it doesn't cross your mind that this will be good training in denying yourself personal desires in order to accomplish something more important. Keeping a promise to help your grandmother move—even after finding out it's the day of the beach party—might not conjure up thankfulness for the chance you have to learn faithfulness.

We're all too accustomed to trying to get out of work, guarding our comfort zones, and taking the easy way out.

Yet, one of the most rewarding decisions you can ever make is to acquire diligence and faithfulness. Is it important enough to you so you'll pay the price—sticking at the things you don't like doing, consistently handing in your homework, honoring promises, and being willing to do disagreeable work? It's your choice.

5. Imitate the servant attitude of Jesus.

Jesus washed His own disciples' feet. He had compassion on the multitudes—even when He was dead tired. In sweltering heat He walked from town to town, when He could have spoken a word to create a beautiful white horse or produce the world's first four-wheel-drive jeep. He and His disciples didn't hang out at Mediterranean resorts. Instead, He put in long days teaching the people, healing their illnesses, and solving their problems. "For even the Son of Man did not come to be served, but to serve, and to give his life as a ransom for many" (Mark 10:45).

If you claim to be a follower of Jesus, you can't shirk responsibility, look for the easiest jobs, ignore the poor, consider the person with problems a nuisance, or take the biggest piece of cake. Jesus taught us to go the extra mile, which literally meant carrying a Roman soldier's gear twice as far as required by law. After lugging the heavy load for a guy who represented foreign oppression, it meant a two-mile hike back to where the person started. In its strictest interpretation, going the second mile means doing a lot of extra work—going beyond what's expected. And it's the secret of enjoying what you're doing.

The girl who does the super book report adding illustrations enjoys it a lot more than the guy who grudgingly just gets by. There's a special satisfaction in not only volunteering to help the elderly neighbor lady mow the yard, but offering to weed her flower bed or trim the shrubs as well. Putting forth the extra effort to decorate the cookies you promised to bake for the kids in Vacation Bible School makes you feel good. Your willingness to be a servant blesses others—and the benefits are returned to you.

God is recruiting Christians with servants' hearts. Sign up. You won't regret it.

6. Decide to do your very best—always.

You probably don't stop to realize that every piece of work you turn out is really an offering to Jesus. "Whatever you do, work at it with all your heart, as working for the Lord, not for men" (Colossians 3:23). He may not especially appreciate the English theme (with seven spelling errors) that you cranked out on the short bus ride to school. You could have brought honor to His name if your music group had faithfully practiced and tuned your guitars *before* the youth meeting started. However, God may not be totally thrilled with your haphazard attitude and your poor performance. What do you think His reaction is to your promising the new girl a ride home from the youth rally, and then leaving her stranded because you got an invitation to go out for ice cream with the popular kids? Jesus was watching when you skipped out of the car-wash project after working only forty-five minutes, in spite of the fact that you signed up for three hours. Did you ask God for His opinion about your asking your friends over to the house to have pizza and leaving the mess for your mother to clean up?

A lot of attitudes and actions you have to give to Jesus may be just plain tacky. But you don't have to live in the past. God makes available to you His forgiveness and His Spirit's power for change.

First, you need to begin by asking God what things are His will for you. A lot of people overcommit themselves to the point where they can do nothing well. Some base their activities solely on selfish interests and personal convenience. Others follow the crowd and wouldn't be caught dead doing anything uncool. You can avoid these traps by making God's priorities your own.

Second, strive for excellence in all you do. Put your best effort into each homework assignment. Do your Sunday school lesson as if it were to be graded by Jesus himself—it is! Putting your heart into making supper, watching your younger brother and sister, or fixing the faucet means you can present that job to Jesus without being ashamed.

Gaining the reputation as a person who can be counted on to do good work is important not only to your spiritual life but also in your everyday existence. Choose the self-discipline required to be the best student and the best worker possible. This will enable you to glorify God, earn the respect of others, and open doors of opportunity.

✔ Setting Your Goal

Check the problems you face:
- ☐ I can't stand someone telling me what to do.
- ☐ I start a lot of things I don't finish.
- ☐ As soon as something gets boring, I quit.
- ☐ I only study enough to pass and hardly ever put forth my best effort.
- ☐ I'm inconsistent. Sometimes I study hard, and sometimes I don't.
- ☐ My room should be declared a disaster area.
- ☐ I usually try to get out of work.
- ☐ I've hardly ever done extra work because I truly wanted to serve.
- ☐ I don't look for things that need doing.
- ☐ It really bothers me if I end up doing more than my share of the work.
- ☐ I argue with my parents, trying to get out of work around the house.
- ☐ I try to disappear if a job needs doing.

___

With God's help, I intend to make the following changes:

_____

_____

_____

_____

_____

_____

Signed, _____

13
A Goal to Last a Lifetime

Why Not the Best?

Sometimes the tragedy of a life is that the person has reached his or her goal. In a high school English text, I read the story of a lady who, as a girl in her early twenties, swam the English Channel. She matured into a rather unattractive and undistinguished woman. She suffered from a health problem that was directly related to her refusal that day to give up and climb into the boat when her body signaled that it was time to quit. She had reached the other side and had enjoyed the admiration and applause of the world—for a while. But one moment of glory wasn't enough to bring her lasting fulfillment.

There are so many people who get rich, marry the person of their dreams, become famous, or graduate with honors— only to find that their achievements leave them with an empty feeling.

All of us need to establish some short-term objectives— to earn an *A* in English, to clean out all our drawers, to make the volleyball team, to attend the youth retreat, to buy a new winter jacket—but we must also set a lifetime goal. Failure to aim at the right finish line causes frustration and confusion.

There is only one worthy lifetime goal: It's a purpose you can pursue no matter what happens to you. It is a goal that will help you reach all your other objectives. It is a goal that you will never fully reach because it always presents new challenges.

Do you know what this goal is?

Jeremiah 9:23–24 will give you the answer:

"Let not the wise man boast of his wisdom or the strong man boast of his strength or the rich man boast of his riches, but let him who boasts boast about this: that he understands and knows me, that I am the Lord, who exercises kindness, justice, and righteousness on earth, for in these I delight," declares the Lord.

And Jesus said:

"Now this is eternal life; that they may know you, the only true God, and Jesus Christ, whom you have sent." (John 17:3)

The incomparable goal is getting to really know God. Like a romance, getting to know God deepens as time goes on. God is so wonderful that the more you know about Him the more you want to know.

☑ Discover for Yourself What God Is Like

First of all, check to see if what others have told you about God is true. Just because someone tries to make you adopt certain "Christian" standards by threatening that God will punish you, don't conclude that He is out to *zap* you. Another may assure you that God is full of *smooshy* sentimentality, or that He'll always let you off the hook so you can do whatever you like. But maybe she doesn't know what she's talking about. If your Uncle Bob finds God hard to get along with, don't decide that it's God who is unjust.

Before you swallow theological nonsense, read the revelation that God himself has given us—that is, the Bible. *Choose to discover for yourself what God is like.*

Although the wonderful world God made gives us some clues about His character, God has chosen to reveal himself to us in two more important ways: through the Bible and through His Son, Jesus Christ, who came to earth and took on human form.

It can totally change your heart to search God's Word, looking for insight about the nature and personality of God. Over and over again you'll see His mercy, His love, and His patience. I would have left the Israelites in the wilderness, destroyed Nineveh, and replaced big-mouth Peter with someone more discreet. But God is the God of the second chance.

He's also a God who can't stand sin and who thinks that eternity is infinitely more important than the here and now. People who never would have come to God anyway were destroyed in a great flood in order to allow mankind to start over again. Pharaoh's arrogance and defiance caught up with him. Idol worship always brought terrible consequences—and still does.

As you spend lots of time reading the Bible and investigating the character of God, you'll discover more about Him.

☑ A Real God Deserves a Real Response

Each attribute and action of God deserves a response from you. When the person you're getting to know says, "I'm president of the senior class," you're expected to say something appropriate. The great work of God and His impeccable character can only call forth our admiration, praise, and worship. When a little kid was asked to write a letter to God, he came up with the following: "I went to see your Grand Canyon this summer. Nice piece of work!" We could learn something from that boy. Many times we don't even react to His fantastic creation, to all He's done for us, to His marvelous plan of salvation, or His mighty deeds throughout the ages. But learning to respond to every insight we have about His character will deepen our relationship with God.

The guy who's in love with a girl praises her long blond hair and beautiful eyes. He compliments her efforts and tells her that her flute solo was super. He comments on the fact that she's patient and caring, and suddenly develops a keen interest in her hobbies. He encourages her in her goal to become a nurse, and laughs at all her jokes. Getting to really know her and become part of her life is top priority—and it fosters a close relationship. People who continue this kind of commitment throughout their marriage begin to think and act very much alike.

If you decide to find out more and more about the character of God and respond to each discovery appropriately, you'll start to think His thoughts, pray His prayers, and live His kind of life. This takes time and effort. There are no shortcuts. But the results are well worth the investment.

A philosopher has said that each of us has a "God-shaped vacuum" inside. If you don't learn how to appreciate God and react appropriately to Him, you'll find yourself going googly over some popular rock star, paying homage to an oriental guru, or sacrificing yourself for a political objective. Man was made for worship and he has invented kings, emperors, czars, and gods of wood and stone. Falling in love, others have made that special someone the object of their worship—until they have a cold, disillusioning experience.

You should save *all* your worship for God. Notice His creation, and praise Him for each thing He has made. Uncover His attributes as you study Scripture. Check out how He carefully prepared Moses for a tough job, and thank Him that you're in His training program for future usefulness in His kingdom. Read about the deliverance of Shadrach, Meshach, and Abednego from the fiery furnace, and praise God that He'll protect you at school. Realize that Solomon knew God's principles well, yet failed to live up to them—and determined to put God's Word immediately into practice.

☞ Make Friends With Your Bible—and the God of Your Bible

Studying the Bible needs to be more than an academic intellectual exercise: It should change your lifestyle. Being able to name the twelve apostles is not nearly as important as deciding to follow Jesus the same way they did. Spouting off everything God created on the fourth day doesn't give God as much pleasure as your being fully able to appreciate the majesty of the One who put the stars in place. What kind of fish swallowed Jonah makes less difference than marveling at the fact that God is God, and that He can do what He wishes.

As you read the Gospels, *fall in love with Jesus.* Thank Him that He had enough compassion to heal a leper, and that He cares about you and can solve your problems. Treasure the purity of motives in Jesus that just had to denounce the Pharisees for their hypocrisy—and take the message to heart. Adore Him for voluntarily bleeding and dying on that old rugged cross so that you can have forgiveness of sins. Praise Him for promising the thief hanging next to Him hope in paradise, and rejoice that He has gone to "prepare a place" for you.

Join a Bible study group, enroll in a course on Genesis, listen to sermons on the radio, be the most serious student in your Sunday school class, take notes in church—do everything possible to learn all that Scripture teaches you about God. But never let what you learn become just a bunch of facts. God is a real Person. Respond to each thing you learn about Him with worship, praise, thanksgiving, confession of sin—and resolve to let Him transform your life.

✔️ Spend Time Just Appreciating God

Biblical worship was never something a person did for one hour a week within the walls of a certain building—it has always been an integral part of life, as it should be today. There are times when worship is rather boisterous. ("Clap your hands, all you nations; shout to God with cries of joy," says Psalm 47:1.) This is a *spontaneous-sports-fan* way of showing your admiration for God. On other occasions worship is a deep peaceful faith. ("Be still, and know that I am God. I will be exalted among the nations, I will be exalted in the earth," says God in Psalm 46:10.) Like a couple in love who just sit in silence enjoying each other's company, we sometimes simply adore the God who made all we see around us: "How many are your works, O Lord! In wisdom you have made them all; the earth is full of your creatures," declares Psalm 104:24.

We can also praise God by recalling all He has done in the past: "Remember the wonders he has done, his miracles, and the judgments he pronounced," says Psalm 105:5. Work is also part of worship: "And whatever you do, whether in word or deed, do it all in the name of the Lord Jesus, giving thanks to God the Father through him," advises Colossians 3:17. When you study for a test or complete a disagreeable job presenting your efforts as a love offering to Jesus, you will experience a great freedom from competition and stress.

We can adore God by constantly thanking Him for everything: "Always giving thanks to God the Father for everything, in the name of our Lord Jesus Christ," commands Paul in Ephesians 5:20. Thanking God for the morning sunshine, for the clothes you put on, for the doughnut you quickly downed for breakfast, for a brain that works normally, for a phone call from a friend, for a chance to sit by the window and read your Bible with no police surveillance—these are invitations for

God to share time with you. Thank God for enough money to go shopping, for the energy to play volleyball, and for your mother's smile. Thanksgiving will help you keep your mind on Jesus.

Important as these *components* of worship are, none can replace public worship: "Let us not give up meeting together, as some are in the habit of doing, but let us encourage one another—and all the more as you see the Day approaching," says Hebrews 10:25. Put your heart into the worship service at your church. Pay attention to the words of each song and listen to everything your pastor says. There is something especially exhilarating about joining with others in praising God. The psalmist captures this excitement: "Glorify the Lord with me; let us exalt his name together," exclaims David in Psalm 34:3. Worship is not just something you do in church—it's a way of life.

Considering the many aspects of worship, you've probably already noticed your weak spots. The following ideas can help you put more worship into your daily life:

1. Read a psalm, making each verse personal. Then use it as a pattern, and make up your own psalm of worship. I recommend Psalms 143–150; 37; 107; 95–100; 86; and 25.

2. Make a list of all the great things God has done for you in the past and say "thank you" for each one.

3. Go for a walk, preferably in a natural setting, thanking God for each flower, puppy, cloud, patch of grass, tree, or person you meet.

4. Sit down and thank God specifically for each thing you own.

5. List all the attributes of God you can think of and praise Him for each one.

6 Sit in silence, receiving His love and appreciating Him.

7. Buy some praise music tapes and listen to them every day for two weeks.

8. Sit down with a hymnbook or a Christian songbook and spend an hour singing praises to God.

9. Choose an appropriate place and time to shout your sports-fan type praise to God.

10. Finish the job you hate most, praising God as you work and giving it as a love offering to God.

As you constantly praise God and realize how great He is, coming to Him in prayer will be the natural way of handling every problem: "Do not be anxious about anything, but in everything, by prayer and petition, with thanksgiving, present your requests to God," Paul tells us in Philippians 4:6.

Learn to pray about every decision. When you go shopping, ask God to help you find a stylish pair of blue jeans at a reasonable price. Consult Him about the best way to study for the exam. Tell God you want Him to improve your personality, and pay attention to what His Word says about attitudes and conduct. When you've been let down, pour out your heart to Him. When you're discouraged, receive His enthusiasm for life. If you don't have any money for the things you need, pray that God will supply it—and expect a miracle. Ask Him to help you give the oral report without being nervous and to play your best in the game. When you get a bad grade, bring your disappointment to God.

Getting to know God better—through study *and* life experience—is the only goal that can last a lifetime. If you don't make this your number one objective, you'll miss out on a whole lot.

☑ Setting Your Goal

It is my intention to make worship a part of my daily life.
Signed, _____
Note the things you plan to do to establish worship habits in your daily life: _____
_____
_____
_____

_____
Signed, _____

Things I plan to do to get more out of public worship:
_____
_____
_____
_____

Signed, _____

14
Formulas, Foresight, Failure, and the Future

When the Going Gets Tough the Tough Get Going

The biography of a champion goes something like this: Jill had always dreamed of winning the Olympic gold medal in figure skating. She took lessons as a child and spent hours each week on the ice. When she fell from a horse and broke a leg, at age twelve, she heard her doctor say that her chances of being a star were gone.

But Jill would not give up. With incredible effort, she became even better than she was before. At fourteen, she entered her first important competition. Although her opening moves were very good, a nasty fall put her in last place. But a year later, she took first.

Then she contracted hepatitis and had to miss six months of practice. Competing while she was still weak, she did very poorly.

Refusing to be discouraged, she undertook an even more rigorous training program. Although she tripped in her first Olympic performance, she returned four years later to take the gold.

The story of another girl with equal talent might read as follows: When Jennifer was three years old, she got a pair of skates for Christmas. Her unusual talent was soon apparent to all. Her parents sought out the best teacher in the city. After a couple years, though, Jennifer lost interest. In the winter, she went skating a lot with her friends, but never practiced seriously. One night a bunch of junior high guys were goofing around and skated straight into her path. She fell so hard that she got the wind knocked out of her and broke two ribs. Fearing another accident, she didn't even put on a pair of skates for three years. Later, Jennifer decided to take a few lessons. Just when she was beginning to prepare for competition, she met Mark and decided that he was more exciting than the ice arena. When they broke up, she opted for the gymnastics team because it was the more popular thing to do.

Obviously, the difference between Jill and Jennifer is that Jill had a clear goal in mind and decided to go for it. In spite of setbacks, she persevered, and finally achieved her goal.

Looking back, Jill could point to the decisions that made an Olympic gold medal possible—going to skating practice when she didn't feel like it, coming back after breaking her leg, pressing on in spite of a last place finish, declining invitations from friends in order to spend more time on the ice to perfect her moves, and even giving up a vacation trip to California so she could keep in shape. The Olympic gold medal represented the sum total of these decisions.

Do you see it? Just a few different choices can change the outcome of your whole life!

It's so easy to pick the option that's the most comfortable or most exciting *at the moment.* In the short run, a chocolate malt is more appealing than a slim figure, lying on the couch watching TV is easier than showing up at basketball practice, and meeting your friends at McDonald's is a lot more fun than staying home to study for the geometry test. The wild party can seem more appealing than prayer meeting, and dating the non-Christian more attractive than hanging around with the girls—unless you consider the possible disastrous future consequences. Going along with the crowd beats telling the principal that Jim called in the bomb scare and taking all the heat from his friends—unless you feel more responsible to God than you do the kids at school. Watching the funny but sexually provocative video might win out over organizing a picnic if you don't really value pure thoughts.

It's been observed that "the easy way makes both rivers and men crooked." Very seldom is the least difficult choice the best one.

The Big Picture

You can never dedicate your life to making the excellent choices that will secure your future unless you have a firm grasp on the big picture. Correct decisions result from knowing God's purpose for you and understanding why it's better than anything you can come up with yourself. Your Creator ought to know what would make your existence fulfilling and meaningful. He is a whole lot smarter than you are. For this reason, choosing God's will is always best.

In order to gain a little more insight into how you can cooperate with God's purpose for you, consider the following principles:

1. *The purpose of life is for you to get to know God and to prepare you for heaven.* Aligning your life with His will is the smart game plan.

2. *God gave you the freedom to choose—and most of your decisions either draw you closer to Him or lead you farther away.* Although it's rarely popular, the option that will keep you near to God is always worth it.

3. *God's will about many specific things is revealed in the Bible.* Scripture also sets forth principles that cover a lot more territory. If your choice goes against God's Word, you can be sure it's a bad one.

4. *As you sense more and more the direction of God's calling on your life, make decisions that line up with this long-range goal.* Study the subjects you'll need in order to be a missionary, a teacher, a carpenter, or a computer programmer. Don't date the person whose purposes are opposite to yours. Don't go so far into debt that you narrow your options.

✔️ Bouncing Back After a Mistake

Although there are no formulas that guarantee right decisions on every possible issue, considering these principles, studying your Bible, praying, and asking the advice of mature Christians will go a long way in eliminating wrong choices from your life. As you set your goals for making the excellent choices that will shape a godly and fulfilling life, you need to be realistic enough to plan for failure.

And what will you do if you blow it? Knowing how to deal with blunders and disappointments is a key to successful living. Great men and women of God knew how to handle mistakes and heartbreak, and you can learn from their examples.

When the Gibeonites staged the first mascarade party in

recorded history and told Joshua they had come from a far country to sign a peace treaty, Joshua fell for it hook, line, and sinker.
The Israelites thought that only someone who was brain-dead
would be able to swallow such a tall tale without even checking
it out.

But we know that Joshua didn't waste time calling himself
names or going into depression. After the enemies of these
Gibeonites attacked them for making peace with Israel, Joshua
led the army to a great victory. He even prayed that the sun
would stand still so they could finish the battle. Talk about a
comeback!

When you do something dumb—and all of us do—reread
Joshua 9 and 10 for a little encouragement. Use the apostle
Paul's formula: "Forgetting what is behind and straining toward
what is ahead, I press on toward the goal to win the prize for
which God has called me heavenward in Christ Jesus" (Philippians 3:13–14).

Mostly-meek Moses really lost his temper in the constantly
complaining company of desert dwellers he was forced to hang
around with. Although God had instructed him to speak to a rock
in order to satisfy a thirsty crowd of Israelites, he gave it a
couple of whacks: "Water gushed out, and the community and
their livestock drank. But the Lord said to Moses and Aaron,

'Because you did not trust in me enough to honor me as holy in the sight of the Israelites, you will not bring this community into the land I give them' " (Numbers 20:11–12). Even though he thought God was making too big a deal out of his disobedience, Moses continued on course. He never threw an if-I-can't-enter-the-promised-land-forget-it tantrum.

Some people let the fact that their failure or their sin keeps them from a certain position or level of respect dampen their enthusiasm for God's work. Don't ever let that happen to you. Don't permit blunders to obscure your objective.

I'm sure that King David would have done anything to erase the actions which began one evening when he went up on the palace roof to relax. Beautiful Bathsheba, palace passion, unsuspecting Uriah, and nagging Nathan changed his life forever. The chaos that reigned in his family was a direct result of his sin. Although it would have been so much better to have avoided the wrongdoing in the first place, David did handle his sin correctly: He admitted his error without blaming anyone else and repented completely. Accepting the punishment and scars as just, he didn't wallow in if-I-only-had-it-all-to-do-over-again wretchedness. He returned immediately to his original goal—that of seeking and serving God with all his heart. He did not permit his miserable detour to derail him from his lifetime objective.

If you sin, don't let the devil convince you that God can never use you again, so you might as well give up. Return to the Lord at once with a new determination to serve Him even more fully.

It's important that you make up your mind to concentrate on *obeying God each day and following Him wholeheartedly*—not on your preconceived notions of "success" or your dreams of accomplishing great things for Jesus. Many people have condemned themselves to failure, have become discouraged, and dropped out, when God was perfectly pleased with their obedience. They quit because they set standards for themselves much different from God's. Don't fall victim to self-induced failure—but if you do, listen to God, let Him restore you, and go on obeying. Let Him comfort you, too, and bring new joy into your life every day.

Keep your goal—to seek God, obey Him, and serve Him

with all your heart—constantly in mind.

Decide that no failure or tragedy can stop you.

Then yours will be the biography of a spiritual champion.

God has provided for failure—including full forgiveness, encouragement, renewed strength, and revived faith. He's given us His Word with its guidelines for forming winning attitudes and making excellent decisions.

Choose to go first class. It's the kind of life God has planned for you! Trying to get toothpaste back into the tube and other similar stunts will not be necessary if you make godly decisions the first time around.

Things That Will Keep You From Trying to Get Toothpaste Back Into the Tube

☐ Am I making the best use of my time?

☐ Am I dealing correctly with all attitudes of bitterness and unforgiveness?

☐ Am I getting God's perspective on my physical appearance?

☐ Am I obeying authority and making appeals when I feel my authority is wrong?

☐ Am I tithing and praying about the way I spend my money?

☐ Do I value human life by taking good care of my body and treating all people equally?

☐ Am I sticking with the practical suggestions that will help me maintain chastity until marriage?

☐ Am I staying clear of all ideas that offer me a formula for God-like power?

☐ Am I constantly taking steps of faith so God can teach me to be a better Christian witness?

☐ Am I studying hard and doing my best work?

☐ Am I worshiping God by praising Him every day?

☐ Am I keeping my eyes on my goal to follow Jesus completely?